HOW A BABY CHANGED MY LIFE

HOW A BABY CHANGED MY LIFE

Compiled by Phyllis Evans

Cover photograph by Barbara Campbell
Design by One Plus One Studio, New York City

ISBN 0-940212-08-0
Copyright © 1982 by American Baby Books.
Printed and bound in the United States
of America
Published by American Baby Books
Wauwatosa, WI 53226
Published simultaneously in Canada

TABLE OF CONTENTS

INTRODUCTION

Who can better understand the joys and frustrations of parenthood than another parent. *How A Baby Changed My Life* is a collection of essays written by expectant and new parents. In their own touching words, mothers and fathers relive pregnancy and childbirth experiences, reveal the myriad emotions involved in being a parent, tell how they solved a parenting problem, or express their feelings about raising a handicapped child.

Each of these stories originally appeared in the "My Own Experience" column in *American Baby* Magazine. This monthly feature is one of the most popular in the magazine, which tells us that expectant and new parents enjoy and benefit from reading about other parents' experiences in addition to sharing their own. We hope that this book will help you cope with the sometimes overwhelming and always challenging responsibilities of parenthood and spark new insights about your own feelings and emotions.

If you have a story that you'd like to share with us for possible publication in *American Baby* Magazine, send it to: "My Own Experience," c/o American Baby Books, 575 Lexington Avenue, New York, New York 10022. (Stories should be typewritten, double-spaced, and accompanied by a stamped, self-addressed envelope.)

The Editors
American Baby Books

CHAPTER 1

PREGNANCY AND CHILDBIRTH EXPERIENCES

A LITTLE PIECE OF DACRON

By Beverly Lahr

"Even the term 'incompetent cervix' seemed to be a reflection on my capabilities as a mother, and it was hard to accept that the 'incompetent' referred only to a small part of my anatomy and not to me as a person."

Although it was a typical, wet, dismal January day, I felt it would take a lot more than the Pacific Northwest rain to dampen my spirits. I was six months pregnant with my second child, feeling terrific, and eagerly looking forward to the April addition to our family. With a little time to spare before my appointment for my monthly checkup, I thought I would stop at the shopping center.

Browsing around the infant's department, I had to muster up a great deal of restraint to keep from buying one of the myriad of cute pink dresses confronting me. With a four-year-old son, I thought it would be nice to have a little girl this time; but like most mothers I was more concerned with having a healthy, normal baby than with what sex it would be.

As I wandered from store to store, I could feel the baby stirring, giving me a little thump now and then to remind me of its presence. But I also was becoming conscious of another, rather vague feeling—sort of a downward pressure. Walking toward the car, I was puzzled by what I felt. There was no pain or discomfort, only the sensation that the baby was about to fall out.

Lying on the examining table, I told my obstetrician about the strange feeling I had experienced just before coming to his office, and he said, "Well, let's have a look." Watching him pull off his glove and drop it into the waste container, I knew that something was wrong. His usually cheerful countenance was one of concern, his casual manner now more serious. But I still was not prepared for his words—words that would cause any uncomfortable mother-to-be in her *ninth* month to heave a sigh of relief, but chilling words to one just barely at the six-months' stage. "It's very likely that you will go into labor within a few days," he announced. While I sat there in stunned silence, he went on to explain, "You have a condition known as an incompetent cervix. The cervix is partially dilated, and the bag of waters is protruding. I can feel the baby's head through the cervix."

His manner was calm, but I felt myself becoming less and less calm. My first pregnancy had been so easy; labor was very short and the delivery quick and easy. "But everything has been fine, just like the last time. How could this happen?" I asked, confused and disbelieving.

"Normally the cervix remains closed throughout pregnancy until labor starts. But if the cervix is damaged in some way, it may not be able to bear the pressure of the growing fetus and uterine contents, and it dilates as the pressure increases," he explained.

A damaged cervix. My mind was able to focus on just one thought—what had I done that caused the damage? A feeling of guilt surged over me, and I searched my memory for that "something" that I must have done wrong. The fall on slippery pavement a couple of weeks ago? The swimming and exercises I had been doing? Lifting my son? Intercourse? Fighting back tears, I asked what I had done wrong.

"You haven't done anything wrong—except maybe have a baby who was in a hurry to get here the first time you were pregnant." Although Dr. Howard had not delivered my first child, he knew from my records that my labor and delivery had been exceptionally fast for a first birth. "Once in a while during a rapid labor, the cervix is damaged. It doesn't show up until the next pregnancy, when its weakened condition prevents it from doing its job. I think that's probably what happened in your case."

I still felt it necessary to recite the list of possible causes that my imagination had so readily supplied with the first pangs of guilt. He assured me that the fall, the swimming, lifting, had absolutely nothing to do with my present state, and I was somewhat relieved. But the release from the sense of responsibility only allowed new and equally disturbing thoughts to emerge. If I went into labor now, this baby hardly had a chance to survive. The tears I had been trying so hard to restrain burst forth.

Dr. Howard was talking to me again, his quiet voice trying to focus my attention on what he was saying. "There are two ways we can try to deal with your condition. One is complete bed rest. Stay off your feet, keep the pressure off the cervix. Sometimes it works. The other alternative is a surgical procedure that involves putting a suture in the cervix to hold it closed until the pregnancy reaches term. There still is some risk that you will go into labor immediately because the surgery itself may induce labor. If we don't follow one of these routes, you are going to have that baby in a matter of days." He wanted me to stay in bed for 24 hours and then meet him at the hospital where he would be on duty the next day; he'd check me again before deciding on surgery.

I dressed slowly, trying to keep my thoughts on what he had said about saving the baby, rather than on what would happen if I went into labor now. I called my husband, asked him to come home with me, and told him I'd be at his office in a few minutes to pick him up. To his question, "Honey, what's wrong?" I could not reply.

Driving to Dean's office, I wondered how he would react to the very real possibility that we might lose this baby. I thought he would just hold me and say, "Don't worry. Everything will be OK." But it didn't work out that way. The combination of my silent phone call and then the tearful description of my visit to the doctor left him almost as scared as I was. He held me all right, but he didn't say, "Everything is going to be OK."

Once I was settled in bed, I began thinking about what it would be like to stay in bed for three months. Our families were 1,200 miles away so who would help out? Friends and neighbors would lend a hand, but three months was too long to expect them to keep us going. We couldn't afford to hire someone to do the cooking and cleaning. Someone had to pick up Randy at nursery school and take care of him until Dean came home. Even the dog needed someone to look after him. I was sure I was too indispensable to my family to be lying in the bedroom while they were left to fend for themselves for three months.

Lying there alone, I tried to sort out my jumbled feelings. In spite of Dr. Howard's assurance that this was not the result of any neglect or misdeed on my part, the guilt feelings that welled up in his office had not completely left me. Even the term "incompetent cervix" seemed to be a reflection on my capabilities as a mother, and it was hard to accept that the "incompetent" referred to only a small part of my anatomy and not to me as a person. But overriding any other emotions that I had was the one most difficult for me to cope with—fear. It was not just a fear that we might lose this baby we so dearly wanted, but also the fear that if it survived, it would never have the chance to realize its full potential because it had been forced out of its maternal environment too soon.

Dean brought in a tray with my supper. What he offered me looked like a picture out of some magazine. I was even more surprised when I discovered it tasted as good as it looked! Maybe I wasn't so indispensable after all.

When Dr. Howard examined me the next day, the cervix had dilated even more, so staying in bed for three months was not going to work, although I had made up my mind to do it if that's what he advised. He called my husband into the room and explained to both of us that he wanted to insert a suture around the cervix to reduce it to its normal size for this stage of pregnancy. It's done through the vagina, so there is no abdominal incision. The Shirodkar procedure takes its name from the Indian physician who developed the technique. The suture works sort of like a drawstring to keep the cervix from opening. When the pregnancy reaches term or labor begins, the suture is removed, and the baby is delivered normally. Or the suture can be left in place and the baby delivered by Cesarean section.

Again he cautioned that there was some risk that I would go into labor anyway, but when we pressed him for some indication of how great a risk, he said that of the dozens of sutures he had put in, only one patient had gone into labor. *That* was encouraging.

When I was wheeled into my hospital room after the operation, the nurse said, "Oh, you're the Shirodkar, aren't you?" She gave me the impression that she had seen quite a few "Shirodkars" before, and that did a lot toward helping me stop feeling that I alone had been singled out among millions of women to have an incompetent cervix.

As the spinal anesthesia wore off, I was surprised that I felt absolutely nothing abnormal in the pelvic region. Dr. Howard had told me that I wouldn't feel the suture or even be able to tell he had done anything. Two days in the hospital, ten days in bed at home, and then I would be free to wait out my pregnancy with my baby held in place with a piece of dacron.

Dr. Howard warned me that it was likely that I would not make it to term, but each day that the baby remained in its uterine environment, it was increasing its chances to live. Each day became sort of a milestone—all those complex mechanisms required for survival had been given another day to mature. I was thrilled when I reached the end of 32 weeks. Just a few more weeks and the baby would have better than a 90 percent chance of survival.

My husband's parents came to help out a month before my due date, and we all waited through several weeks of sporadic contractions that produced no results. As the baby grew larger those last few weeks, I could feel pressure on the suture—not the horrible feeling I had experienced in the shopping center that day—just a feeling of pressure that made walking somewhat uncomfortable.

When I went in for my checkup a few days before my due date, I complained to Dr. Howard, "You did such a good job keeping this baby in, I'm beginning to think it's never going to come out. Are you *sure* I'm going to go into labor with that suture in there?" He laughed and said that if the baby didn't make an appearance within a week after my due date, he would take out the suture.

Even a trip to see a scary movie on my due date didn't jar the suture. Just before the delivery Dr. Howard asked if I'd like to keep the suture as a souvenir. Looking at the bloody thing he had just removed, I said, "Heavens, no!" He ruptured the membranes, and a few hours later Brady Lee arrived, a hefty and healthy 8 lbs. 9 ozs.

Several times in the last few months I have looked at this smiling, happy baby and rather wished that I had kept that suture. An Indian physician, a very competent obstetrician, and that little piece of dacron saved our baby. ☐

ANOTHER CHANCE

By Cherie Aldana

*"It was true that I wanted another child more than anything,
but the fear of being hurt again, of losing another
baby, weighed heavily on my mind."*

I had just finished bathing Michael, my two-and-a-half-year-old, and was reading a bedtime story. I was one week short of entering my seventh month of pregnancy, but this was a Friday, and Friday meant a day of strenuous housecleaning. I always felt a great deal of satisfaction when these chores had been completed. My husband, Al, was working late, but he'd be home soon, and with Michael in bed, we would be able to enjoy a quiet dinner by ourselves.

A feeling of relaxation was finally beginning to settle in, when a sudden hot gush escaped from my body. I ran, terrified, to the bathroom. Aghast, I saw bright red blood pouring from within me. My thoughts ran rampant! My baby, my baby! Please—let me feel the kicking that I love so much! I couldn't bear it if anything were to go wrong now. Frantically, I telephoned my obstetrician, who advised me to go to the hospital at once. I desperately wanted to stay home, in the safety of my bedroom, away from the bad news I felt certain awaited me in the hospital. But when I called Al and told him what had happened, he convinced me that the doctor was right.

I packed a few things as I waited for Al, and I prayed. An hour later I was in the hospital being examined by my doctor. My baby was fine, he said, but it wasn't until I began to feel the baby's kicking that I actually believed him. The bleeding continued, though, and I remained in the hospital, confined to my bed, for eight days. During this time the doctor stressed the importance of remaining calm and not letting my fears overwhelm me. How could I possibly "keep my cool" when with every move I made, I could feel the gushes. By the time I left the hospital, the bleeding had just about subsided, but my doctor cautioned me to stay in bed, at home, for the duration of my pregnancy.

A sonogram, which is a method of scanning the uterus (or any other part of the body) through the use of sound waves rather than x-rays, had confirmed my condition to be *placenta praevia*. This is a complication that presents itself in the third trimester of pregnancy. The problem is that the placenta has attached itself to the uterus, below rather than above, the baby. It is the pressure of the growing fetus on the placenta that causes the bleeding. The doctor explained that there might be additional hemorrhaging, but that hopefully we would be able to control it without further hospitalization. I also learned that since a baby must be born before the placenta is discharged, a vaginal delivery was out of the question. By performing a Cesarean section, however, the doctor could deliver the baby before the placenta, and he was optimistic that all would be well.

During the next two months, my life changed drastically. My husband, my mother, and my sister completely took over caring for Michael and running the household. They saw to it that I remained in bed around the clock and followed doctor's orders to the letter. It was difficult not to worry, and my anxiety and fears seemed to multiply in my idleness.

On a Wednesday, the day before I entered my ninth month, I was told by the doctor that my Cesarean section was scheduled for the following Monday. "Thank God," I said, thinking of the day when I would at last have my baby and once again lead a normal existence. I was aware that I had become obsessed with fear about the culmination of this pregnancy. My thoughts were concentrated only on the moment when I would be able to hold my baby and hear my doctor telling me what a fine, healthy infant I had. Monday...Monday...Monday... it couldn't come fast enough for me. I didn't know as I went to sleep that night, dreaming of Monday, that my pregnancy wouldn't even last till then.

The following morning, I awoke at 5 a.m. with what I thought was a labor pain. Two hours later, I knew that I was indeed in labor. I called my doctor, and he said he would meet me at the hospital. Later that morning, our second son was born. I remember waking up and feeling so glad that my ordeal was finally over; I was unaware that the real ordeal was just beginning.

About 3 p.m. my doctor came to see me in my room. Still very groggy from the medication I had been given, I didn't realize the ramifications of what he was saying. The baby had had some difficulty breathing shortly after he was born, and he was now on a respirator in the intensive care nursery. My doctor explained that although this was not a usual complication of my condition, it was, nevertheless, possible that the two were related.

Al came in later that afternoon, and though he had seen me shortly after the baby was born, he hadn't wanted to upset me by telling me of our son's difficulties. He had hoped the situation would soon improve and that he could spare me further anguish. When I told Al that the doctor had been in, he understood that I now knew the truth. I asked him to check with the nursery to find out how our son was progressing. He was gone for quite a long time, and it was then that I realized just how serious the baby's condition must be.

My fears were soon confirmed when Al returned to my room along with the doctor in charge of the intensive care nursery. They told me that the baby's breathing problems had become much worse and that they did not expect him to pull through. The next few hours seemed like a film in slow motion with Al running back and forth from the nursery to my room to give me the latest reports. When he came into my room that last time, the tears were welling in his eyes, and there was no need for him to tell me what had happened...

I soon learned how much it could hurt to lose someone you never even knew. But my baby had been so much a part of me for all those months that I felt as if I actually had known him. I had talked to him, prayed for him, worried about him. On the surface it appeared that my life had returned to normal, but the ache I felt inside never faded. It just seemed to grow greater with time. A day did not pass that I didn't relive the whole episode in my mind. I enjoyed being able to once again care for Al and Michael, whom I loved with all my heart, but there was an ever-present emptiness that just wouldn't go away.

A few months later, I visited my obstetrician for a checkup. Afterwards, we had a lengthy discussion about what had happened to me, as he sensed that I was still quite troubled. I recall asking him, "When does the emptiness go away?" He answered, "Only after you have filled it—by having the baby you really want." He said that if I had always planned to have more than one child, then by all means, I should try again. Medically speaking, it was still possible for me to have another baby, but he explained that since the cause of my previous complication was unknown, there was a slightly greater risk that the same thing could happen again.

In the weeks that followed, I thought of nothing but what he had said— both the positive things and the negative. It was true that I wanted another child more than anything, but the fear of being hurt again, of losing another baby, weighed heavily on my mind. I talked with other women about their pregnancies whenever I had the opportunity. In a way, I suppose, I was seeking an answer—some guidance, some wisdom, some hope, a guarantee, perhaps— anything that would show me the right direction.

One evening at a nursery school meeting, several mothers and I were talking about pregnancy. To my surprise, I found that many of the women had survived experiences far worse than mine. As I listened to their stories, my emotions overwhelmed me. I was filled with admiration for their strength and disappointment in my own weakness. I realized that I had been so saturated with self-pity and doubt, that I had been oblivious to the fact that I was not the only person ever to have suffered tragedy. For the first time since my loss, I felt something positive surging through me. I saw that other women—women just like me—had found the courage to overcome their hurts and their fears and had tried again for the babies they so desperately wanted. It was incredible how I had let fear paralyze my life for so many months. "Not anymore," I silently vowed.

My decision was finally made, and eight weeks later, my doctor verified the fact that I was pregnant. There were still some fears, deep inside, but the hope and the anticipation far outweighed any negative thoughts I had. I felt marvelous, and everything progressed beautifully. Each day I was thankful to be having such a normal, uneventful pregnancy. This time I was taking things much easier. I didn't have to do as much for Michael, as he was now quite an independent little boy of three and a half. Al helped with the housework, and I was really able to get a great deal of rest.

As they wheel me down the corridor to the delivery room, I pray that everything will be fine. I see my doctor, and he smiles down at me reassuringly. My eyes reveal how very scared I am. I fall asleep then, and what seems like only a few moments later, I am awakened. My doctor is at my side, telling me that I have a healthy, beautiful son. The words repeat themselves in my mind. My heart is just bursting, and I cry, letting the tears of happiness and love drench my face.

A few hours later, Al and I, together, meet our new son for the first time. The nurse hands him to me, and he cuddles into my arms as if he knows how very much I love him. The thrill is indescribable. I kiss his face, and I am filled with peaceful contentment. The emptiness has gone. □

CESAREAN: A LOVELY WAY TO HAVE A BABY

By Carol Webster

"I thought of my girl friend's suggestion to 'be prepared,' and at that moment I was ready. I felt no disappointment that I would not have natural childbirth."

My baby was two weeks overdue, and our family, friends, and neighbors had begun to call daily to ask if I had felt any labor pains yet. One evening my girl friend called, and we had what turned out to be a prophetic conversation. She had delivered her first child by Cesarean just two months before. She had called to tell me to be prepared in case my doctor recommended a Cesarean during my labor. She said it was not an unpleasant experience at all, but a lovely way to have a baby. As it turned out, less than 24 hours after that conversation, my baby was born by Cesarean.

From all the books I read during my pregnancy, I knew that more than 10 percent of deliveries were Cesarean but that the odds were against my needing one. Besides, early in my pregnancy my obstetrician had measured my pelvis and had told me to expect a normal delivery. Although friends joked about my "narrow hips," I knew it wasn't the exterior width that mattered but the distance between the ischial spines that was important.

My labor was relatively easy and painless. I awakened very early in the morning with a strange sensation in my lower abdomen. I went into the bathroom and noticed the "bloody show," a sure sign that labor had begun. When my husband asked anxiously from the bed, "Is this it?" I told him that indeed it was "The Day," but that I felt fine and there was no need to hurry to the hospital.

I crawled back into bed, happy that our baby was finally on its way, yet wanting to savor the last few hours my husband and I would be alone in our home. We waited for almost an hour and began to practice our breathing techniques. I then felt my first labor pain and asked Chris to rub my lower back. The sensation came again and again, although irregularly. I was so absorbed in trying to stay calm and doing my breathing, that I hadn't noticed that my husband had been timing contractions. He insisted that we go to the hospital, but I thought there was no need to rush. As soon as I got to the bathroom to put on my makeup, I realized that I would be lucky if I could just change from my nightgown into clothes. Standing up had become very uncomfortable, and all I wanted to do was lie down again.

As soon as we were admitted into the labor room, they examined me and announced that I was already dilated eight centimeters. I realized that I must have gone through the first stage of labor in my sleep and had only awakened as I was about to reach the transition phase. With Chris right beside me for moral support and for backrubs while I did the breathing exercises, I didn't feel any pain that I couldn't handle. "It's really a case of mind over matter," I told my husband, and we were both thankful that labor was going so easily.

Later that morning the obstetrician was called. I was fully dilated, and after he examined me, he said that I could begin to push. My husband lifted my back and counted while I held my breath and bore down. At the other end of the table the obstetrician was telling me to push. My husband began to tell me to push too. I thought to myself that the situation was like a football game with the roles reversed: I'm the "athlete," and they're the cheerleaders. I was ready to start laughing, but they both seemed so serious that I decided against it. After some time, it no longer seemed so funny to me. I had been trying to push the baby out for almost an hour, and yet the baby wasn't making any progress. Finally, the obstetrician suggested a caudal. He said that I would quickly get exhausted pushing, and he wanted me to be able to push without any pain or tension. He also said that it might be necessary to use forceps, and he wanted me to be prepared.

Even though my husband and I had wanted and planned for a natural childbirth, we weren't disappointed when a caudal was ordered. I hadn't been in any pain, but I was getting tired and hungry. It had been almost seven hours since I had first awakened and started breathing exercises. The baby's heart was being monitored, and we knew that he wasn't in trouble, yet we were concerned that he wasn't born as quickly as we had expected.

From our reading and from our natural childbirth classes, we knew that a caudal was one of the least harmful anesthetics to the baby, and we knew that Tacoma General Hospital was well known for their expertise in administering caudals. I had imagined that injecting the caudal might be painful, but it wasn't bad at all. Soon I began to feel a numbness in my legs, similar to the feeling of novocaine. In fact, after a while I couldn't feel the contractions at all, and a nurse had to tell me when to push.

We had been in the labor room all day when the obstetrician suggested a Cesarean. "I think we should take the baby from the top," were his words, and at first we didn't understand what he meant. When he explained that the baby's head appeared to be too large to pass by the ischial spines, we quickly agreed to a Cesarean. I thought of my girl friend's suggestion to "be prepared," and at that moment I was ready. I felt no disappointment that I would not have natural childbirth. I suppose that having spent hours in labor made me eager for the birth of our child, and the method by which he was born became less important. What was important was that he would be born soon and would not suffer from a long labor and possible oxygen loss.

Now things moved quickly. I was taken to the operating room, and Chris stayed behind. The catheter was already in place, but the effects of the anesthesia would wear off before the Cesarean could be completed, so more anesthesia was injected. Because I was already numb, I couldn't feel the fluid being injected. While the obstetricians washed up, one of the nurses gave me a marvelous massage on my bulging stomach and then applied a local anesthetic. The anesthesiologist introduced himself, and I asked questions about the caudal and its effects.

I was fully awake and talking with the doctors during the whole operation. I had expected to feel a tingling sensation when they made the incision, but I felt nothing at all. You can imagine my surprise when I heard my baby cry, and the doctor announced that I had a healthy baby boy. The nurse brought my baby to the head of the table so that I could see he was absolutely perfect and then took him several feet away in order to do the Apgar tests. My son continued to cry, and I began to cry tears of joy. I overheard the doctor give an Apgar score of 9, and I was relieved to know that he would be fine.

Later, when my husband and I were together again on the maternity floor, I asked if he was disappointed that he wasn't with me during the delivery. He told me that all during my pregnancy he had worried that something might be wrong with our child. He said he knew he would have just broken down and cried in the delivery room if anything had gone wrong, and that he wouldn't have been able to give me support. I told him that I wasn't in the least disappointed either, so in spite of our preparations for natural childbirth, the Cesarean had worked out very well for me.

The most difficult thing about having a Cesarean was how to respond to the people who expressed sorrow for us because we couldn't have natural childbirth. Having used the breathing techniques in labor, we knew the value of natural childbirth preparation, and we didn't feel we had missed out on anything. Knowing that a Cesarean can prevent a prolonged labor and possible brain damage to the newborn due to oxygen loss, and that it is a safe operation for the mother, we were happy that it was a viable alternative to natural childbirth.

Now I find myself calling friends who are pregnant to give them the same advice my girl friend gave me the night before our son, Marc, was born. I tell them to read as much as they can about childbirth, to take classes on natural childbirth techniques, and to be prepared in case a Cesarean becomes necessary. You may not think you will need a Cesarean—I certainly didn't—but keep an open mind. And don't be afraid; it's a lovely way to deliver a baby. □

CHILDBIRTH 14 YEARS AGO AND TODAY

By Arthur Featherstonhaugh

"The difference between this child's birth and those of the others was that I felt a deep sense of achievement, a joy of welcoming a new life into the world, a closeness to my wife, and a mutual love that I had never felt before."

"**H**oney, better get up now! I think we ought to start." My wife was standing beside the bed, almost dressed and trying, but not succeeding, to look calm.

"OK darling...be with you in a minute," I said as I stumbled into the bathroom to shower and shave. I was torn between a feeling of relief at the arrival of this moment and one of regret that I couldn't crawl back into bed for another eight hours. However, as the spray of hot water wakened me, relief—and excited anticipation—began to win out. At long last our baby was signalling its arrival.

It was to be our first child, and her first child, but not *my* first child. Asleep in the house were four other children, ages ten to fourteen, from my first marriage. My second wife, Dina, had elected to marry me *and* the children. But because Dina wanted to have her own baby, and because I loved her and wanted her to, we did.

And the children were eager to have a new brother or sister.

As Dina bent over the oldest—a boy, fourteen years old—to give him final instructions on what to do in our absence, I couldn't help remembering that morning almost 14 years ago when I had nervously embarked on a similar errand.

The doctor had told Alice, my first wife, that she was due "soon" and that she should come in at noon the next day "if nothing seems to be happening earlier." After a fitful night for both of us, we got up about 7:30 a.m. I had placed my confidence in the old idea that when you are in labor, you'll know it. Well, I wasn't in labor, Alice was—and she *didn't* know it.

Since she seemed uncomfortable, I suggested that she call the doctor, and I went out to start the car. We had a 45-mile drive to the hospital, and I figured I'd let the car warm up while I shaved and had a quick cup of coffee; then we'd have a leisurely drive over the winter countryside to the hospital. But no sooner had I inserted the key in the ignition than I saw Alice, wild-eyed and uncombed, emerging from the front door. "But," I sputtered, "I haven't even brushed my teeth! Can't I at least shave?"

"Goooo...ooOOH!" she moaned. I went, gas pedal to floorboard, while poor Alice tried to crawl from the front seat to the rear and back again, all the while crying, moaning, and asking for help. When we got to the hospital, she was taken straight to the labor room while I took care of admission. After I signed her in, I was allowed into the room for a few minutes. By this time Alice was in a panic, lying in a hospital bed, all alone and waiting for something to happen to her body that had never happened before and over which she had no control.

Not that she was ignorant. Alice was a brilliant woman, and she'd read extensively about the birth process. She could have described it as accurately as any obstetrician. But she had never experienced it or been prepared to experience it in any way but the traditional one of pain and tension. Centuries of fear did their work, ably assisted by the nursing staff, some of whom seemed to take a perverse pleasure in "initiating" a new sister into the ancient sorority of female suffering. Anxiety, discomfort, uncertainty, and isolation reinforced one another. I was there, it's true, but what a weak reed to lean on! My contribution was to murmur, "There, there...," or "It'll be OK," without the least idea whether it would be. I couldn't do anything to help.

Mercifully, Alice must have been in transition to the final stage of labor even as we left the house, for after a very short time, they wheeled her away from me and into the harsh glare and terrifying furnishings of the delivery room. As they took her away, one of the nurses said, nastily, "Doesn't feel as good coming out as it did going in, does it?" I was appalled—and angry.

I realized that in addition to everything else, Alice had to bring forth her firstborn without any female sympathy. That nurse obviously held some part of the view that the pleasure of sex must be paid for by the pain of labor. And, of course, the corollary of such a view is that nothing can be done to relieve the woman's anguish, short of rendering her unconscious. It all seemed unfair to me, and I could hardly bear to think how that nurse's remark must have affected Alice.

A half-hour later, they wheeled her past me in the corridor. She was groggy and barely able to recognize me. A doctor padded out. "It's a boy," he said. "Everything's fine." I went home, cleaned up, ate, collected the suitcase we had forgotten in our haste, and drove back for visiting hours.

A large crowd had collected outside the double doors that sealed off the maternity ward from the rest of the hospital. We waited until platoons of nurses and aides carried the babies back to the nursery. When all the babies had been taken away from their mothers and locked up behind plate glass, they let us unwashed and festering mortals approach our wives.

Alice had found the experience of childbirth to be painful, frightening, and humiliating. She was now frustrated by her experience in the hospital. "Rooming in" was a theory but not a practice then. A mother's desire to breast-feed her child was regarded by the staff as inconvenient, disruptive of routine, and a possibly neurotic aberration that ought to be discouraged. The only woman who was allowed to keep her baby with her had given birth in the ambulance on her way to the hospital—and she, with her newborn, was in isolation.

I found it hard to grasp the reality of fatherhood. I stared through the glass at the fourth from the left in the third row and thought "So?" That red, prune-faced lump had, at that moment, no more relationship to me than any of the other red and brown ones beside him. For the first week of his life, I found it hard to believe in the baby's existence.

Now, 14 years later, another woman and I drove through the brilliant pre-dawn moonlight on our way to the hospital. We were relaxed, hopeful, and happy. Of course, I had been a father four times over; but what, exactly, does having a baby mean to a father? So far, it had meant very little. Had I ever given birth? Had I ever made any contribution, besides taking my wife to the hospital? Did I actually know anything about the birth process? Could I have helped my wife in any real way if I had been called on? The answers were no, no, no, and no.

If I had so little experience with childbirth, why, then, was I smiling to myself this wintry morning? Because this time I *did* know something about the birth process. I was ready to help my wife, and I was going to be there for the whole event and have plenty to do. Whatever Dina was going to do, I would be busy.

The difference? *Preparation.* Dina and I had chosen a doctor who accepted only those patients who wanted "natural" childbirth. Throughout the nine months of waiting, emphasis was on preparation for the birth by both parents. The doctor outlined the ground rules for us at our first interview, and most important for me was to attend each examination during the pregnancy and go to a course in Lamaze training to help my wife during labor and delivery.

I admit I was skeptical as to the value of my presence in the midst of all this. After all, *I* wasn't going to have the baby. The only experience I'd ever had of Lamaze was a film I'd seen once describing Dr. Lamaze's ideas. The film featured an on-camera birth that embarrassed and nauseated me. I was sure that I would faint at a critical moment, leaving the doctor, midwife, and nurses to stumble over a 190-pound body placed strategically at the center of things.

I needn't have worried. I didn't faint. I was far too involved and interested. Furthermore, I knew exactly what was happening to my wife, what to expect and when to expect it, and what *I* would be expected to do.

To my surprise, my role as a supporting actor turned out to be crucial for my wife's comfort and confidence. After checking into the hospital, a quick examination revealed that we had a long way to go, so we were sent out to take a walk. Walk we did—after lunch, after dinner, and as night came on, we walked around the ward. The midwife didn't come until 1:30 a.m. and the doctor not until 2:00. We were still walking, very slowly, at 5 a.m., so tired that we occasionally drifted off to sleep while standing up. Whenever Dina lay down, the contractions stopped, so we remained on our feet. When the hard contractions hit Dina, I hung on to her and helped her count to regulate her breathing. When the pain of back labor came, I applied counterpressure. I was there, never away from her side, except to prepare more tea in the small kitchen.

When the baby began to descend the birth canal, 24 hours after labor had begun, we sat Dina down. I held the mirror so she could see, the midwife watched the progress, and the nurse monitored the fetal heartbeat. The doctor sat, sipping coffee, benignly watching Dina's efforts but ready to whisk her to the empty delivery room at the first sign of trouble. (That was never necessary; we were able to remain in the birthing room.)

By 7 a.m. we had a full house as we moved Dina to the bed: the doctor (who was on his feet now), the midwife, the nurse about to go off duty, the nurse just coming on, and me. As the midwife gently massaged Dina's perineum (to prevent tearing), I placed pillows under Dina's knees, and with her back propped up, we were ready for the final moments. As I stood back to photograph the actual birth, in one climactic push the baby's head appeared. The doctor suctioned out his mouth and nostrils, and 30 seconds later, there he was, quite suddenly, turning pink and gloriously alive.

The doctor looked at him quickly and then put him on his mother's stomach until the umbilical cord stopped pulsing. Then I heard the doctor say to me, "You have another job to do!" I looked up to see him holding a pair of scissors, indicating the point at which I was to cut the cord. The baby was put to his mother's breast for a few moments, and then the doctor instructed me to remove my shirt so that I could hold the minutes-old baby on my bare chest. As the doctor and midwife assisted the delivery of the placenta, my fully conscious third son stared solemnly into my face as his tiny, perfect fingers twined themselves tightly in the hair on my chest. Dina spent the rest of the day relaxing and getting acquainted with the baby. I left after a while to carry the good news to my four children whose births I had not witnessed.

They say that fathers are more closely bonded to children whose births they see, but I don't think so, at least not in my case. I love all my children. I have bathed, diapered, fed, burped, and doctored them all. The difference between this child's birth and those of the others was that I felt a deep sense of achievement, a joy at welcoming a new life into the world, a closeness to my wife, and a mutual love that I had never felt before.

The two birth experiences, 14 years apart, were polar opposites. Dina experienced, as my first wife had not, a happy (albeit still painful) and lovingly supported childbirth. And for the first time, I had been given a share in a key event in the life of a family—I had helped bring my child into the world. Finally, I belonged. □

COPING WITH MISCARRIAGE

By Susan Grier Phillips

"I felt empty...My mental time frame for the next few months, once full of plans, hopes, and dreams, now seemed a big, dark, sad blank. I felt as if there was little to live for."

I was three months into my first pregnancy and on cloud nine. Everything was going so smoothly. The nausea I'd felt earlier had long since disappeared, I had plenty of energy, and I hadn't gained a pound.

The first hint that something might be wrong came at my 12-week checkup, when the doctor failed to pick up a fetal heartbeat. I was disappointed, but since the doctor didn't seem overly concerned, I didn't give it a second thought. I was told to return in two weeks for another try.

Two days later I began spotting—so lightly I was almost embarrassed to call the doctor. His nurse instructed me to rest in bed and report any changes. The spotting was minimal and only a faint brownish color. There was no cause for alarm, I knew, unless it became bright red. Nevertheless, I dreaded telling my husband, John. I didn't want to face the reality that something might ruin my so-far perfect pregnancy.

That night the dreaded change came—the spotting became bright red. John telephoned the doctor while I lay in bed, still stubbornly refusing to believe that anything serious could be happening. I was shocked when he hung up and informed me that we were going to the hospital.

This was not what I had envisioned. It was months too early to be going to the hospital, my belly was supposed to be huge, and John was supposed to be excitedly timing contractions. Instead my still-flat tummy suddenly seemed empty of all its hopes and dreams. The silence we shared en route to the hospital was still emptier.

I was placed in the hospital maternity ward, and my condition was listed as threatened abortion. My room was the last one on the hall, farthest away from the heart-tugging cries of the nursery.

Being tucked away like that was, of course, a blessing. As I later learned, it also represented the attitude most of us have toward miscarriage. The subject is carefully tucked away—in books, hospitals, and our minds—where we don't have to face it. For those who never have to confront miscarriage, that's fine.

However, such a way of thinking and acting, I found, makes coping with miscarriage much harder than it should be.

It was three long days before my own miscarriage occurred. There was still very little bleeding but a lot of pain. It started with a slight backache, building up into faint contractions that finally became so strong that I honestly thought I was going to die—and wouldn't have minded. With only a vague knowledge of the Lamaze method we were so looking forward to, I was totally unprepared to handle this fierce, gripping pain. Fortunately, the hospital allowed John to stay beside me, holding my hand and providing me what little support he could. When the doctor arrived, my cervix was completely open, but the uterus had not yet expelled its contents. The pain mercifully stopped—only temporarily, the doctor explained—before they wheeled me into the operating room for a D & C to finish nature's course.

When I awoke less than an hour later, I was enveloped by a drowsy sense of well-being. The absence of that terrible pain seemed blissful. I knew I had lost my baby, but at this point, my only emotion was a sense of relief. At least the ordeal was over.

It wasn't until John deposited me back in my own bed at home the next day that it began to hit me. In the hospital I had felt secure and cared for. But at home, in the rooms where we had dreamed and planned for the new arrival to our family, I was overwhelmed by the loss.

The first few days were hard, but at least I was sheltered somewhat in my own little world at home. Friends called, one or two dropped by, and cards and flowers arrived from out-of-town relatives. In that protected and loving world, coping with the miscarriage did not seem an impossible task.

But when I returned to work three days later in an effort to bring my life back to normal as soon as possible, I began to realize how deeply the miscarriage had affected me and how long the road to emotional recovery was going to be. Physically, I was fine. I tried hard to put on a strong outward appearance, but inside I was devastated.

I felt cheated that miscarriage had happened to me. I knew the statistics proved that miscarriage is very common, but why me? And why did it have to happen with my first pregnancy? I was sure that no other pregnancy would ever hold the special starry-eyed magic I had felt with this one.

It seemed unfair that I should lose the baby after all the care I had taken to ensure a healthy and strong pregnancy. I had sworn off coffee, pushed away even the smallest cocktail, cut back on desserts, and faithfully attended my weekly ballet class.

I knew that my miscarriage was not caused by anything I did or did not do. Like many first trimester miscarriages, mine was simply the result of a blighted ovum—an embryo that, for chromosomal reasons, fails to divide and multiply properly. I knew that well-meaning friends and acquaintances were absolutely right when they tried to comfort me with statements like, "Be glad." "It was for the best." However, not much rational thinking was going on in my head at the time.

I felt empty. I missed the feelings of well-being and anticipation that I had had during the pregnancy. My mental time frame for the next few months, once full of plans, hopes, and dreams, now seemed a big, dark, sad blank. I felt as if there was little to live for.

Worst of all, the miscarriage left me feeling very lonely. Few people seemed to understand what I was going through. Many people simply withdrew, uneasy with fears of not knowing what to say. A friend from back home confided to my sister, "I wanted to write and say I was sorry, but I didn't know what to say." It wouldn't have mattered to me what she said. Just knowing she cared would have been enough.

There were those who did provide touches of the care and support I so desperately needed. Many were women who had gone through miscarriages themselves. The simple words, "I had one too. I know how you feel," were the most comforting and reassuring I heard. One friend who had never been pregnant provided immense support. She visited me in the hospital, cooked dinner for my husband, called to check on me every day after the miscarriage, and later helped plan outings to get my mind off my troubles.

It was weeks before my spirits lifted. One day about two months after the miscarriage, I noticed that I was laughing and that it felt good. I hadn't felt so free in a long time. It was still longer—months—before I began to feel like a whole person again. But the miscarriage left its mark on just about every aspect of my life, from my work to my relationship with John.

They say the best healing for the emotional trauma of miscarriage is the joy of a new pregnancy. Happily, I can report that this is indeed true. But I wasn't able to breathe easily until I had passed that 12-week mark that stopped me in my tracks the first time around.

Now that we have heard the baby's heartbeat and felt those first thrilling movements of life, the pain of last year's miscarriage seems farther away, replaced once again by the wonder of pregnancy, childbirth, and motherhood. □

GRANDMA GOES TO LAMAZE

By Amanda Geisler

"Throughout my labor she encouraged me in the way that a football coach would cheer on his team. She made me feel positive that I could control the pain, and I did."

A husband's delight at the announcement of an expected baby, the sharing and planning during a pregnancy, the final excitement of a successful delivery—most women dream that these feelings will be a part of their first pregnancy. For me, as for many others, the reality was somewhat different. My husband and I separated in the second month of my pregnancy. Though I wanted the baby, I was frightened and confused by the changes taking place in my life. With apprehension I faced the fact that a stranger was coming into my life and a familiar confidante was leaving it. Thanks to Lamaze and a wonderfully supportive mother, my pregnancy and delivery were memorable experiences instead of the disasters they might have been.

When my doctor first suggested that I attend a Lamaze course, I was dubious. I thought Lamaze was something a husband and wife did together. However, I was eager to experience a drug-free childbirth, and, as my doctor pointed out, one only needs a partner, not a husband. My mother was thrilled to act as my partner and was extremely curious to find out what goes on in a delivery room. (She had not seen any of her own babies born because of hospital policies 25 years ago.)

As we walked into the first session of the Lamaze course, my heart sank. As I had feared, all the couples were man and wife. But the friendliness and enthusiasm of the instructor quickly put me at ease. In the confusion of that first evening's introductions, most of my classmates must not have realized that my mother and I were partners. One man exclaimed upon meeting my mother, "Why you hardly look pregnant at all!" She was not sure whether to accept this remark as a compliment or an insult.

For me, the Lamaze course offered an extremely supportive experience. No one questioned my situation or made me feel uncomfortable. To my surprise, having my mother as a partner was actually an advantage. Initially, we both felt rather foolish doing the floor exercises with the other couples, but it soon became apparent that my mother was better equipped to simulate timing contractions and to massage areas that would be tense, since she had experienced labor pains herself. She became an integral part of the education process in that class, as she was able to relate her childbirth experiences to all of us first-time mothers. Aside from the Lamaze techniques, the course provided me with such an exhaustive supply of information about pregnancy and delivery that I felt no anxiety at all about the experiences ahead of me.

I also made many close friends through the class. During pregnancy every development is extremely interesting to the pregnant woman but much less so to her friends and relatives. With no husband to talk to and discuss the minutiae of my symptoms, or such things as the baby's first kick, these friends became invaluable because of their real interest in pregnancy. It was heartening to discover that others experienced indigestion, sleepless nights, and lower back pains, and to trade remedies for these ills. Association with other pregnant women is like belonging to an exclusive club, and it compensates for those times when one feels excluded from the interests of friends who are not pregnant.

My labor began after midnight when I was awakened by the leakage of some water. I shilly-shallied around, not certain that I was actually in labor. Since I had been out to an elaborate dinner that evening, I thought that my rather mild pains might be attributed to overeating. After taking a shower, putting on makeup, and making sure my bag was packed, I sat down and timed my contractions. They were five minutes apart. I phoned my parents, who awakened instantly and sprang into action. For the past week my mother had slept with her hospital outfit set on a table beside her. They were at my house in minutes.

The hospital was only a short drive away, but by the time I was in the wheelchair and on my way up to maternity, the contractions were three minutes apart and much stronger. It was becoming apparent that my mother and I were not going to need the books and cards that she had brought along in anticipation of a long wait. That night the hospital was flooded with pregnant women and badly understaffed. Since there was no one to prep me when we reached the labor room, we started the Lamaze exercises.

During the period that followed, the importance of the Lamaze partner was made real to me. There was no labor room nurse available, and I relied completely on my mother to help me concentrate and control the waves of pain. At one particularly uncomfortable point, she was massaging my lower back and I snapped, "That's not doing a bit of good!" Fortunately, she did not take offense at this, as she had been well educated by the Lamaze course to expect such testiness during the transition phase. Throughout my labor she encouraged me in the way that a football coach would cheer on his team. She made me feel positive that I could control the pain, and I did.

In what seemed like an incredibly short time, I felt the urge to push. When I informed my mother of this, she left me to locate a nurse. Though she was gone only a few minutes, I felt my resolve slipping and was doubly grateful when she returned. When the nurse examined me, sure enough, I was fully dilated, and the baby was ready to be delivered.

My doctor could not be located, and a substitute rushed in at the last minute. As we careened down to the delivery room, I crossed my legs and willed away the impulse to push. Once in the delivery room, everything seemed to go wrong. No obstetrical nurse was available, and as I looked around, I noted signs on the infant warmer and the fetal monitor reading "Out of Order" and "Broken." Worst of all, the wedge used to prop up the laboring mother was missing. My own mother stepped into the breach and propped me up with her arms. With each push, I strained back against her. Of the two of us, I think she had the harder job. After half an hour of pushing, my daughter, Chessa, was born. The labor and delivery had lasted a total of two and a half hours.

Though conditions at the hospital were far from ideal, I had barely noticed them. The intensity of my partnership with my mother and the excitement of the birth of my child drove all trivial considerations from my mind. My daughter's birth was a joyful and sharing experience for me and my mother. I was fully conscious throughout the whole process and was able to feel and view that awesome and breathtaking voyage of a baby into the light. My mother had the rare opportunity to watch her first grandchild come into the world.

For any woman in a situation similar to mine, I would highly recommend the Lamaze course. Having somebody with you who is educated about and involved in the birth can make all the difference in your feelings about your delivery. If you are widowed, divorced, unmarried, or even if your husband is overseas or scheduled to be away on business, find yourself another partner. It can be a relative or close friend. Don't hesitate to ask them to help you out. Remember, you are doing them a favor, too, by offering them a "once-in-a-lifetime" opportunity to assist in what must be one of life's most rewarding events. I'm sure you will find that they are flattered and eager to assist.

A woman's dream of pregnancy culminates in the moment when she holds that new life for the first time and gazes at the miracle that is her child. For me, the dream's happy ending was fulfilled one hundred times over.   □

HUSBANDLESS CHILDBIRTH

By Nancy Dean

"...I would probably have to go through labor and delivery on my own. However, I felt that if I planned well, I could handle it when the time came."

"Well, this is it," my husband announced excitedly one day in March. "The promotion came through. I'll start as regional manager in Milwaukee on April 1." I felt my fingers turn icy. This was what Steve had always wanted and what I had wanted for him, but the timing was poor.

I was six months pregnant with our second child. It was a long-awaited pregnancy as I had had two successive miscarriages after the birth of our son, now age four. I was also a gestational diabetic and would have to be watched closely during my last month of pregnancy. The thought of selling our home, making a major move, finding a new doctor with whom I could feel confident—all while my husband began a new job—seemed overwhelming.

I decided then that I could best cope with the situation by remaining in Dayton until after the birth of our baby. It would give me time to adjust to the idea of a move and would also give our son more time to accept it. I would feel much more relaxed knowing that Aaron would be with his grandmother during my hospital stay, rather than with a stranger in a new city.

I knew that because of this decision, I would probably have to go through labor and delivery on my own. However, I felt that if I planned well, I could handle it when the time came.

The company complied with our wishes and allowed Steve to commute on weekends. The first three weeks were the worst. Off Steve went on Monday morning, suitcase in hand, bubbling with anticipation. I felt deserted. He was setting out to conquer new worlds while the highlight of my day would be helping Aaron with his bath.

All the minor problems of the day turned into major ones without Steve around to listen to me complain in the evening, and all the household chores seemed monumental without him to help share the load. I found myself ranting and raving about the smallest things, like taking out the garbage. I began to feel resentful. Was my husband more excited about the new job than the new baby? Was he out meeting beautiful new people while I sat home looking like a walrus? Was I doing all the work while he was getting all the glory?

By the fourth week I had picked myself up and polished off my sense of humor. I had a lot to accomplish in a short time, and self-pity would simply not fit into my schedule. Moreover, I became aware that Steve was dealing with many pressures too. He was feeling his way in a new job while trying to find enough time to be a good husband and father. I decided that he didn't need my complaining. I feigned confidence to reassure him, then felt it begin to grow.

I found that the best therapy was keeping busy. First, I put the house up for sale, and after many tense moments and endless visits from prospective buyers, it was sold. I got out as much as possible to attend La Leche meetings and a childbirth refresher course. I worried that I would feel uncomfortable going to the course alone but managed to feel quite at ease and enjoyed it thoroughly. I practiced my breathing exercises nightly and went to bed feeling smug.

I knew Steve would be able to be with me during labor if it started between Thursday and Sunday evenings. I decided to assume that I wouldn't be that lucky, and I planned accordingly; that way I would be fully prepared and not feel disappointed when the time came.

June came and with it my due date. My visits to the doctor increased. Twice a week I was hooked up to the fetal monitor for stress testing. Contractions were initiated, and the monitor gave an indication as to how the fetus would undergo the stress of labor. Then off to the lab for an estriol count. I was getting anxious for D-Day.

Our first child had been born a month prematurely. Now with two weeks left until due date, I already felt overdue. My first labor had been so easy that I had only known it had started because of the spotting. I was afraid that once again I would not recognize the contractions until the last stages of labor, and I hoped I would make it to the hospital on time.

My fears were well-founded. On Wednesday, I was aware of contractions all day, but they felt like the same Braxton-Hicks contractions I had experienced throughout my pregnancy. I did not feel uncomfortable, so I chose to ignore them. I had read that if a woman was in true labor, she would not be able to sleep all night. That night I slept like a log. The next afternoon Steve called to see if all was well. He thought I would have the baby soon and wanted to try to catch an earlier flight home. I assured him that I would still be around for the weekend. After I hung up, I felt ravenous. That was proof I wasn't in labor! I polished off a huge lunch with gusto then decided to be productive. In went a load of laundry, and out came the vacuum cleaner.

Early in the afternoon I put Aaron down for a nap. Then my water broke, and I felt the first contraction that was the real thing. Another one followed four minutes later, with heavy bleeding. I knew now that things would move quickly.

Fortunately, my younger sister, home from college, was visiting with me at the time. She was able to stay with Aaron while I contacted my neighbor who had planned to be my surrogate "husband" if needed. She had just finished washing her hair when I called. I picked up my suitcase and headed next door just as she was backing her car out of the garage, her hair in dripping ringlets.

The ride to the hospital could only be described as harrowing. There was a digital clock on the dashboard, and I watched it religiously. As we sped onto the freeway, I noted that my contractions were only two minutes apart. I used the Mack truck ahead of me as my focal point and breathed easily. I let my body go totally limp and could barely feel the pain. I kept chattering excitedly between contractions.

The rest of the trip was like an episode of *I Love Lucy.* We took the wrong exit and were hopelessly lost. As we neared the downtown area, I noted that my contractions were a minute and a half apart. I tried to sound nonchalant as I mentioned this to my neighbor, whose knuckles were now white against the steering wheel. She stopped the car to ask directions, and when we finally pulled up to the maternity entrance, I was almost completely dilated.

The question, "What did you eat last and when?" turned out to be an embarrassing one. There I was with a full stomach, about ready to have a baby, feeling no nausea. Moreover, I had been totally unaware of transition. I felt as if I had just taken some time out of my daily routine to stop and have a baby.

Things slowed down in the delivery room as it took me a while to push the baby through the birth canal. But our son was born, healthy and content, a mere 30 minutes later. Needless to say, I had natural childbirth, and I felt fantastic. It was then that I realized that Steve wouldn't even know about Jimmy's birth until his arrival at the airport around 10:00 that evening. It would be almost like telling him I was pregnant all over again.

So much has been written about the joys of childbirth when the husband shares in the experience. We have learned that it often brings a couple closer and strengthens their marriage. All of us who have had our husbands present during labor and delivery know this to be true. Yet little is written about the woman, who for whatever reason, must go it alone. It is often implied that she must have a support person with her or she will falter and that she will probably not enjoy or treasure the experience. To the contrary, I found the birth of our second son to be exciting and rewarding. It enabled me to grow as an individual and as a wife and mother. I had to give up a few things that I would have wanted, but in so doing, I was made more aware of my husband's feelings during this critical time and was better able to share some of his pressures. In the process I became more independent and realized capabilities that were never tested before.

My husband and I also grew closer in a special way. We had learned the give-and-take of a less-than-ideal situation. We had not only survived it but also gained from it.

Now, a year later, I often hear the question, "How did you get through that by yourself?" I find myself smiling like the Little Engine and saying, "I thought I could." ☐

PREGNANCY AFTER FORTY

By Caroline Roberts Pinholster

"...I walked out of my doctor's office, overcome with shock and disbelief. Forty-two years old and pregnant for the fifth time!"

April in Atlanta is a beautiful month. The dogwood and azaleas bloom everywhere you look, and the tall pines form a stately backdrop for the tender new green of budding hardwoods. On such a day I walked out of my doctor's office, overcome with shock and disbelief. Forty-two years old and pregnant for the fifth time! It couldn't be happening. My husband, Garland, and I were parents of four healthy, wonderful daughters aged eighteen, fifteen, thirteen, and ten. We certainly had not counted on this little "caboose."

I walked along in the soft, spring air and sensed a strange little feeling trying to push through my general mood of shock, like a tiny plant pushes up through the earth. It suddenly burst into full bloom and identified itself—it was joy.

In high school and college I had been something of a dilettante of the arts, always writing poetry, painting, trying to express some deep creative urge inside. Then came marriage, teaching, and pregnancy. The moment I saw my first daughter's tiny face, I knew this was the ultimate in creativity. I could never create a poem, a song, or a painting to equal the miracle of new life itself. This feeling grew and deepened as each child came along and I shared in their growth and development. So I was really glad about the forthcoming child, even leaping ahead in my thoughts to more years of chicken pox and Dr. Seuss, bicycles and sticky ice cream, and all the rest.

My husband met the news of my pregnancy by alternating between being horrified and being tickled to death. We discussed all the pros and cons and decided to trust in God and enjoy the whole thing.

Only one cloud loomed on the horizon, and that was the spectre of birth defects. Only a few days before, I had read an article in the newspaper on Down Syndrome. This is a very tragic affliction in which the newborn child has an extra chromosome—47 instead of the normal 46—and suffers a variety of defects, including severe mental retardation. While the causes of Down Syndrome are not fully understood, the article stated that women over forty who give birth run a much higher risk than younger mothers of having a baby with

Down Syndrome. Recent studies indicate a statistical risk of 10 to 12 percent. Knowing this bothered me.

Of course, I discussed my fears with my doctor. He told me that there is a test called amniocentesis, which can detect some defects before birth. Down Syndrome can be detected because of the extra chromosome. He suggested making an appointment for me at Emory University Medical Center in Atlanta to talk over my situation with a genetic counselor.

A few days later I met with the counselor in Emory Hospital. Pleasant and professional, she first took a complete family history from me and my husband. Neither of us has any history of hereditary disease or defects in our large families, so the picture looked good from that standpoint. Then the counselor explained the procedure of amniocentesis and the indications for having the test. The whole field of genetics is incredibly complex. There are several conditions that can now be detected by amniocentesis. The test itself consists of taking a sample of the amniotic fluid that surrounds the baby with a long slender needle. This fluid contains cells from the growing fetus that have been sloughed off. The fluid is cultured and analyzed through a series of complicated tests.

The test, she told me, should be done no earlier than 12 weeks (there is usually no amniotic fluid formed before then) and no later than 20 weeks. If the fetus is afflicted by Down Syndrome, she explained carefully, and if I decided to have an abortion rather than bear the child, it should be done as early as possible. She hoped I had considered the possibility of an abortion. I had. There are times in life, I believe, when the choice is not between good and bad, but between the lesser of two evils. My husband and I had agreed that an abortion would be preferable to giving birth to a severely retarded child. There are those, I know, who would not agree. But this was our decision.

The newspaper article had been correct about the percentage of Down Syndrome in births to women over forty. The test itself is not without a small risk, less than one percent. There have been instances of miscarriage following amniocentesis. But the doctor who would perform the procedure is highly skilled, and he carries out the test several times a week. Weighing the statistical risks, I opted for amniocentesis, and it was scheduled for the following week.

On the day before the test date, I reported to the hospital for a sonogram. This is a relatively new technique whereby a picture of the fetus is obtained with ultrasound waves and the baby is not exposed to the danger of radiation by x-ray. This was completely painless. An armlike attachment was moved back and forth over my abdomen, and gradually the sound waves were converted to dots on a television screen, then to film by a Polaroid camera. I don't begin to really understand the whole process, but a series of pictures was the result. These showed the fetus and its position and would guide the doctor who would perform amniocentesis.

The following day Garland drove me back to Emory for the test itself. I lay, fully dressed, on an examining table. A younger doctor was in the room to observe the technique. The nurse covered me with a clean sheet, then pulled sheet and slacks down to expose the lower abdomen, which she swabbed well with disinfectant. The sonogram had shown I was approximately 17 weeks pregnant. The doctor injected an anesthetic into the skin just above the pubic region. He took a long, thin needle off the table beside me, and at this point I closed my eyes. I have to admit I was a little scared. There was a prick, followed by a feeling like a mild menstrual cramp. "You can usually feel a slight pop as the needle enters the uterus," the older doctor was telling the younger one. I lay very still. It didn't really hurt, and I was less afraid now that the needle was in place. He withdrew some fluid and announced that it was a good, clear sample, so they would not have to try again. (Sometimes, I had been warned, the needle would hit a small blood vessel and the sample would be bloody, so the needle must be re-inserted for another sample.) That was all there was to it. He sponged me with alcohol and advised me to take it easy for the rest of the day and call my doctor if I had any cramping or bleeding. He chatted with my husband briefly and told us the doctor in charge of the genetics lab would call with the results in about two weeks.

The two weeks of waiting to learn the results of amniocentesis were the hardest part of this whole experience. I tried to prepare myself if the news should be bad. I imagined it happening, the abortion and the emptiness afterward. One afternoon I took my daughters swimming and sat sunning myself after a short swim. A couple, in their sixties, arrived at the pool, accompanied by a young man who must have been their son. It was immediately evident that he was a victim of Down Syndrome. Many thoughts went through my mind that afternoon.

At last the call came. The doctor told me with no fanfare, "Good news. Normal chromosomes are present. We find no evidence of any abnormality." Then she asked, "You did want to know the sex, did you not? Some mothers would rather wait and be surprised." I had forgotten that the counselor had told me that amniocentesis discloses the sex of the child. Yes, I wanted to know, although I felt sure it would be another girl. The bright voice continued, "Then perhaps I should say, normal *male* chromosomes!"

This story has a happy ending. Our fine boy is here. I was able to enjoy my pregnancy without anxiety; I even knew what color to paint the nursery. I realize that having a baby after forty is not right for everyone. However, with the growing availability of amniocentesis at medical centers around the country, I predict that more women over forty will be exercising the option of having a much-wanted baby. As for my husband and me—well, it's April in Atlanta. The dogwood is blooming. Sometimes we think our son needs a brother or sister close to his own age. It's a possibility to think about. □

PROBLEM PREGNANCY

By Gail E. Lush

"...I was shaken by the prospect of so many medical tests and a possible lengthy hospitalization. But I felt I had found someone who could give our baby the best possible chance."

The news that I was pregnant again brought mixed feelings. With joy came a sense of fear and anxiety—my first pregnancy had ended with a stillborn son. No reason was ever found, and while the doctors had been encouraging about another pregnancy, they couldn't erase our fears.

When I visited our family doctor for the pregnancy test, she suggested that I get the best medical care possible for this pregnancy. Instead of referring me to the local obstetrician who had handled my first pregnancy, she advised me to consider a specialist in high-risk pregnancies. As a diabetic I was considered "double" high-risk.

At first, the thought of traveling 35 miles to see such a specialist didn't thrill me. Our baby would be due in mid-winter, and I didn't want to be hospitalized that far away. I also wondered how I'd be able to keep my job and at the same time arrange for frequent office visits and medical tests with at least 45 minutes' traveling time each way. But the last thing I wanted was to lose another baby, so I decided to see the specialist recommended by my family doctor. My goal to have a healthy baby would make the effort worthwhile. And if I lost, again, I would know that I had tried my best.

The specialist asked me a number of questions about my medical history and previous pregnancy, and he explained in detail the problems associated with diabetic pregnancies. The mother's diabetes can prematurely age the placenta, which has the job of supplying the baby's oxygen and nutrition as well as removing waste products from the baby's system. In some cases the placenta begins to break down near the end of pregnancy. To avoid this complication and possible infant death, babies of diabetic mothers are usually delivered several weeks early through induced labor or Cesarean births. Medical tests are used during the last weeks of pregnancy to determine how well the placenta is functioning and the best time for baby's delivery. I could expect a number of medical tests during my pregnancy and was also told I might need to be hospitalized several weeks before the baby's arrival.

As I left the doctor's office, I was shaken by the prospect of so many medical tests and a possible lengthy hospitalization. But I felt I had found someone who could give our baby the best possible chance.

My pregnancy progressed smoothly. I alternated visits every two weeks between our family doctor and the specialist, which saved me quite a few trips to the city. And my fears that the pregnancy would interfere with my job were unfounded. I was able to get a number of lab tests done at the local hospital on my way to work. My doctor's appointments were all scheduled late in the afternoon, and when I needed to leave work an hour early, my boss was very understanding.

As my pregnancy advanced, I was able to see firsthand some of the marvels of medical technology. One of the most fascinating tests that is now available is ultrasound or sonogram. This machine produces a picture much like an x-ray, but since it operates with ultrahigh-frequency sound waves, it is completely harmless. My first ultrasound, when the baby was 19 weeks along, showed the baby's heart beating and skeletal development. It was reassuring to see that our baby was growing normally. A later ultrasound at 32 weeks again confirmed the baby's proper physical development and age, as well as giving us a glimpse of him or her thumb-sucking.

I was given estriol counts and nonstress tests. Estriol measurement helps determine how well the placenta is functioning. This has traditionally been done by measuring the amount of this hormone present in a 24-hour collection of the mother's urine, but now a blood test has been developed to measure estriol in the mother's blood. The nonstress test is done by attaching a fetal monitor to the mother's abdomen and recording the baby's heartbeat.

In my 36th week of pregnancy, I entered the hospital. The specialist wanted me under surveillance so that if the baby's well-being was threatened, the delivery could be scheduled immediately. The goal was to give the baby as much time to grow inside me as possible and yet schedule the delivery before major risks developed.

A third doctor, the head of the neonatal intensive care unit (NICU), now entered the picture. He explained that after birth our baby would automatically be admitted to the NICU. Because my blood sugar level as a diabetic ran differently than normal, our baby's blood sugar might be unstable at birth. The baby would be put on a glucose IV for the first couple of days to make sure it stabilized. In addition, because the baby would be born prematurely, there was a chance he or she would develop breathing difficulties. The baby would be kept in the NICU for at least the first several days before going to the regular nursery, and we were relieved to learn that the NICU was well prepared to deal with any problems the baby might have.

In the hospital I also had an amniocentesis test. A small amount of amniotic fluid was drawn out of my abdomen with a needle, and this fluid was tested for substances that show the degree of the baby's lung maturity. The results revealed that the baby's lungs were mature enough for delivery, and a Cesarean delivery was scheduled for the following day.

Two weeks after my admittance to the hospital and three weeks short of term, Karyn arrived. I had spinal anesthesia for the delivery, so I was wide awake and alert yet felt no pain. My husband, Tom, was allowed to scrub up and be with me for the delivery. Tom and I saw Karyn's head emerge and heard her start crying immediately. Tom was able to hold our baby and bring her over to me before she was taken to the NICU.

The specialist's predictions were right on target. Karyn needed some oxygen for the first few hours after birth and was on an IV for the first two days. Three days after birth she was doing fine on her own and was transferred to the general nursery. For the rest of our hospital stay, I was able to have her room in with me during the day. One week after delivery, Tom and I took our beautiful, healthy baby home.

I learned several valuable lessons from my experience. A problem pregnancy takes extra effort and work. It may mean seeking out a specialist for medical care, a longer hospital stay, more frequent visits to the doctor, and more medical tests. But pregnancy is an investment: physically, emotionally, financially, and time-wise. As my doctor told me, "You want to protect your investment as best you can." This helped me realize that there was an end in sight and that the inconveniences were only temporary.

Many of my fears were greatly reduced by getting answers to my questions. Learning the facts about diabetic pregnancies helped me understand both the need for the medical tests I was given and what the results meant. I knew in advance that my delivery would probably be a Cesarean, and I had plenty of time to read a book on Cesarean deliveries, ask my doctor questions, and talk to several new mothers who had Cesarean deliveries. Talking to the head of the Neonatal Intensive Care Unit about what to expect in terms of our baby's condition at birth also helped. I wasn't frightened when I saw Karyn hooked up to an IV because I was prepared for it.

Last, I learned that a problem pregnancy doesn't have to result in a second-rate birth experience. Because our baby was born in a hospital with a progressive, family-oriented atmosphere, the birth experience was a joyful one that Tom and I shared. The personnel in the NICU encouraged as much parent-child interaction as possible, and I was able to breast-feed Karyn as soon as I felt up to it.

Karyn is now a happy, normal three-month old. We are already planning for a brother or sister for her in a couple of years. Problem pregnancies might take more work, but the results are priceless. □

THE RELUCTANT EXPECTANT FATHER

By John B. Corns

"But as Pam bubbled with anticipation, I remained indifferent toward her pregnancy. I thought only of my desires and how a baby would interfere with my pursuit of the good life."

"**Y**ou're what?" I asked in disbelief.

"I'm pregnant," was Pam's reply.

I couldn't believe it. Rather, I did not *want* to believe it. A baby was the last thing in the world I wanted. Pam and I had delayed the starting of a family, and after six years of marriage I had become accustomed to a childless life. Her news sent a shock wave through me that I'll never forget.

Pam feared that the longer we waited to start a family, the more difficult it would be to break away from the *status quo.* She was right. I did not want to change my lifestyle of having fun. And to me children were not much fun. I was not ready for the changes inherent in the arrival of a baby, especially the loss of our free time and Pam's income. Naturally Pam and all of our friends and relatives were delighted at the prospect of a new baby. Pam's positive attitude about the child growing within her caused her to literally glow with excitement, to take a greater interest in life. She had never been so happy, so effervescent, so beautiful.

But as Pam bubbled with anticipation, I remained indifferent toward her pregnancy. I thought only of my desires and how a baby would interfere with my pursuit of the good life. Oh, I knew that I would make a good parent *some* day, but not now. I did not want the added responsibility for another human being or the additional financial burden on my shoulders. A new baby meant that I would have to find a better-paying job, and finding a new job would not be easy in light of the widespread unemployment at the time. Consequently, I worried about money matters and just how we would meet our financial obligations. My attitude changed from indifference to negativism.

As a professional photographer, I was interested in taking pictures of the birth of our first child, in spite of my negative attitude about starting a family. A prerequisite for any expectant father's entry into our hospital delivery room was the attendance at prenatal classes. So reluctantly, I complied with hospital rules and went with Pam to the weekly classes.

In fact, I found the classes very informative. The main premise was to encourage future fathers to attend these classes with their wives so they could learn about the mysteries and beauties of childbirth and to promote a more active role on the fathers' part during pregnancy. We were given a feeling of being needed during the labor and delivery process, a feeling that went against our stereotyped visions of the expectant father nervously pacing in the waiting room. At all times our instructors encouraged participation by the fathers, not only for the mother's well-being but also for the father's.

There was one woman in our class who came alone each week because her husband had to travel on business. One of the class instructors assumed the role of surrogate husband each week so the woman would be able to practice her breathing exercises. This woman said she felt very sad and very alone during class, especially when she saw the other fathers taking part and enjoying it. The sadness in her eyes disturbed me but made me feel good about taking an active role in Pam's pregnancy. My negative attitude toward starting a family prevailed, but little by little I grew to accept the fact that things were changing.

Childbirth films were shown during our course of instruction, depicting in full color some of the gorier aspects of childbirth. Several fathers in our class were disturbed by such sights and vowed never to enter the delivery room. I was somewhat upset, too, and suddenly had second thoughts about going into the delivery room with Pam. Yet I was determined to shoot photographs of the baby's birth and cast all doubts aside. My decision to enter the delivery room was not based on Pam's needs but rather on my selfish desire to get the photographs that I wanted. Pam was not totally convinced by my bravado, and she prepared herself mentally to go through childbirth without me in the event I should back out at the last minute.

A week after her due date, Pam went into labor late one night. It was happening; there would be no turning back now. Everything we had read and studied was about to become reality for us. Still unexcited about becoming a father, I rolled over and went back to sleep, thinking of what I had to do at work the next day.

Fifteen hours later when Pam's contractions were ten minutes apart, we left for the hospital. When we were reunited in the labor room, after the admission procedures, I began to feel the immediacy of the situation. As I held Pam's hand and helped her through her contractions, it suddenly dawned on me that within a few hours I was going to be a father. I had put such thoughts out of my mind for the last nine months, acting as if Pam's pregnancy was some kind of bad dream that would go away. But now, for the first time, it was a nice feeling.

During the next several hours in the hospital, Pam's life was filled with uniformed strangers, each pushing and probing, listening to this and checking that. Every so often someone would reach under the sheet and check on the dilation of Pam's cervix, destroying any sense of modesty she possessed. Compounding the matter were the intravenous needles in her arms and the epidural anesthetic needle in her back. I felt sorry that she had to undergo this ordeal after several months of backaches and other pregnancy-related discomforts.

I thought then of the woman who came alone to our prenatal classes and of her facing the delivery of her child without the moral support of her husband. It saddened me to think of Pam in a similar situation, so I began to take a greater interest in her well-being. More than ever Pam needed me and my words of encouragement. It was time for me to stop thinking only of myself and help Pam with the delivery of *our* child.

Pam responded to my improved attitude. She needed me to comfort her through the pain of labor, to reassure her. As a result, I sensed a feeling of worth I never had before. The emotional bond between us grew very strong, with each of us reinforcing the other's needs with love and positive attitudes. I did my best to be a good husband for Pam and to be a good father for my as-yet-unborn child. I felt ashamed of the way I had acted in the past and began to really look forward to the arrival of our baby.

Periodically I was asked to leave the labor room for reasons unclear to me, and each time I was invited back about 15 minutes later. I later learned that Pam had asked the nurses to shoo me away each time she had to bear down for a contraction. She felt that I might become upset at seeing her endure the pain of bearing down, and to spare me this unpleasantness I was asked to return to the waiting room. After all she had been through with her pregnancy and her labor, Pam was still concerned about my well-being.

"The baby is coming," a nurse suddenly announced to me as I sat in the waiting room. "Hurry, or you'll miss it," she shouted, compounding my already anxious demeanor.

I hopped down the corridor behind the nurse, trying to put on the paper shoe covers, cap, and mask with one hand while grabbing my camera with the other. After all of the preparation for this event, I was afraid that I was going to miss the birth of my first child because of wardrobe troubles.

My pulse was racing, and my respiration came in quick, short breaths. I was anxious to be with Pam again. Many thoughts flashed through my mind, but most of all I thought of how much I loved Pam and the baby she carried. All traces of my poor attitude were gone, and I was ready to go into the delivery room not only to take photos but also to help Pam with the delivery of our baby.

Upon my arrival in the delivery room, the nurse directed me to a bench in the hallway. "Hurry up and wait," I mused to myself. During this wait I tried to regain my composure after the psychological "high" I had just experienced. It was quite a letdown to just sit there, so I spent the time checking my camera equipment and chatting with the obstetrician who would be delivering our baby.

We entered the delivery room and went about our duties. I embraced Pam and offered her words of love and encouragement. Now and then I shot a photograph of the nurses as they readied everything for the delivery. I also checked with the doctor about where I could shoot my photos without getting in everyone's way. Again my pulse and respiration rates quickened.

The emotional level in the room began to rise as the baby's head began to emerge. I tore myself away from Pam's side to begin photographing the birth of our child. My glasses started to fog from my rapid breathing and perspiring forehead, making it difficult to focus the camera. My mind was a jumble of thoughts and feelings again. Was this really happening to us?

Then I saw *him,* our son Brenton, appear before my eyes. The emotional bond between us was immediate, and I loved that little guy from the moment I saw him. I was excited beyond belief—a combination of love, anxiety, and pride. Watching my son entering the world was the most moving experience of my life, and I was so grateful that I was able to witness it.

Brenton was covered here and there with vernix, and he had purplish-colored hands and feet. At first I had trouble realizing that Pam and I were parents, that Brenton was real. But there he was, squirming around before our very eyes. A new life, a new person, my son. I loved him, I wanted him, and I was happy that he was going to be part of our life.

I was torn between holding Pam's hand and speaking with her, shooting photos, and looking at Brenton. I let Pam know how much I loved her and how proud I was of our new son, and then I rushed over to Brenton and spoke with him for a while. I stroked his soft skin and spoke with him as if he were an adult. I was at my emotional peak, feeling a love for Pam and Brenton that I had not known was possible a few hours earlier. Pam and I embraced and cried with joy as Brenton let his presence be known with a healthy cry of his own. Yes, the birth of a child really is a miracle of nature and surely the most beautiful experience in a parent's life.

I left Pam in the hands of the hospital staff and followed Brenton as a nurse wheeled him down to the nursery. Pam was put into the recovery room and left alone for the most part. She felt let down after the emotional high she had just experienced, thinking that the world had forgotten her as she lay there alone. There were no nurses, no new mothers, no husband to share in her feelings of happiness and love. Had I known differently, I would have been at her side, seeing that she received moral support.

I had waited until the last moment to enjoy the experience of pregnancy and childbirth and am grateful now that I finally became involved. I almost missed the most beautiful and moving experience of my life, the birth of my child.

Having been thus converted to the role of a proud and loving parent, I have learned to appreciate fatherhood, to enjoy my son. Therefore, I was not shocked last week when I asked Pam, "You're what?" □

THERE'S MORE THAN ONE WAY TO HAVE A BABY

By Rosina Landis Case

"Yes, our Lamaze instructor had warned that at least one woman in our class would have a Cesarean, but I had only half listened. She certainly did not mean me!"

Even though I was only six weeks pregnant, I began reading every book about pregnancy and childbirth I could get my hands on. For the next six months I read and read and began to have a very good idea of how I wanted this wonderful baby to enter the world. All the books warned of complications, despite prepared childbirth training, that sometimes lead to medication for the mother, or in some cases the need for a Cesarean. I skimmed these paragraphs, as I knew I would have no complications that I could not overcome through sheer determination and will power.

By this time my mind had created a picture of a perfect birth, and I actually choked up with tears every time I dreamed it. It went like this:

Having practiced my Lamaze exercises diligently, I would be in excellent health and would know my breathing techniques better than any previous Lamaze student, thus graduating with honors from my class.

During labor my devoted husband would never leave my side, and we would work together hand in hand through the contractions, oblivious to the people in white scurrying about us. No matter how many hours there would be, I, with the help of my husband, would go the whole ten yards. I would be tired, yes; uncomfortable, granted; but never NEVER, would I so much as ask for an aspirin.

And when our son was born, my husband and I would laugh and cry with the happiness of the overwhelmingly beautiful experience we had shared, as we cooed over and cradled our miraculous accomplishment.

A short time after delivery I would be out of bed calling all my friends. Two days later my husband and I would leave the hospital, babe in arms, riding off into the sunset.

It's not funny. I really knew that's how it would be. I wanted it to be that way, and as time went on, I became desperate for it to be that way.

In the middle of my eighth month, my husband and I started our Lamaze classes. I was ecstatic. Now I could start preparing for my dream delivery. I hung on the instructor's every word. I exercised faithfully but not quite with the ease I had pictured. My husband was very interested in all that we were learning about birth and my body and how I could control and help the natural process of childbirth so as to benefit myself and especially our baby. He was a calm, reassuring, and conscientious coach, and even though I drove him crazy demanding perfection of both of us in the practicing of our breathing technique, he remained patient.

A few weeks before my baby's arrival, I visited my doctor, who examined me and said, "You're going to have a very big baby."

"Will I have any trouble with a Lamaze delivery?" I asked, confident that I would not.

"Don't worry, dear, there's more than one way to have a baby," he remarked as he turned to write on my chart.

Shocked, I almost screamed, "What do you mean by that? A Cesarean?"

"It's *always* a possibility, dear." The door opened, and he was gone.

All my vital signs accelerated into double time. Yes, our Lamaze instructor had warned that at least one woman in our class would have a Cesarean, but I had only half listened. She certainly did not mean me! I wanted so much to be successful with my Lamaze techniques, to meet the challenge of control versus panic, self-discipline versus pain. More than anything I wanted to look at my baby's face and into my husband's eyes and know that I had done my best. So I decided to exercise and practice the breathing techniques extra hard. Since I had obviously chosen a doctor who was an alarmist, I proceeded to put the conversation out of my mind.

But as it turned out, my baby was born a very long two weeks after even my doctor's estimated due date. "He" was a girl, and she was delivered by Cesarean. My husband and I had victoriously handled 19 hours of labor without any medication, but it was determined after all that the 8 lb. 3 oz. baby was indeed too big for my pelvis. I begged the doctor to let me continue according to my plan. He was wonderful, stayed with me for hours, and gave me all the time he felt he safely could. However, my labor was not progressing satisfactorily, and it was a danger to me and the baby to continue.

As I succumbed to the turn of events and the impending operation, I became frantic. Despite my doctor's earlier warning of a Cesarean, I had read nothing on the subject, nor had I asked any of my friends who had gone through it one question. Instead of being prepared as I had planned, I was totally stunned and confused. Things happened too fast, and I lost all control. I had no idea what to expect, and worst of all my husband could not be with me. At the last minute he was taken from my side, and I was wheeled into an operating room and given a spinal. Somewhere in the night a nurse shook me to tell me about my daughter. Couldn't be! I had felt nothing, slept through everything. I did not feel at all like a mother but rather the victim of some awful accident. My husband said that when I was brought up to my room, I had the most disgusted look on my face he had ever seen.

Kristianna was perfect, for which I am deeply grateful, and she's much more beautiful than I even imagined. But I was consumed with an unshakable feeling of disappointment and failure that I had not delivered her naturally. Very depressing to me was the thought that the rest of our children (we want a big family) would be born the same way—terrifying major surgery for me and no husband at my side. I was scared for what I had just gone through and for the next time.

Everyone reminded me over and over that the most important thing was that the baby and I were fine. My mind acknowledged this obvious truth, but my heart continued to feel cheated. All the negative feelings surrounding the birth stayed with me, and I could not find myself.

Months later I continued to rehash the entire event, trying to place blame, direct my anger at some tangible circumstance. I questioned my doctor's judgment, my own womanhood, and even wondered if my husband could have been a better coach. My self-esteem was so destroyed that I could not bear to be with women who had delivered their babies normally. My physical scar had long since healed, and I was certainly back on my feet, but emotionally everything still hurt.

Then one day I heard of a group called C/SEC (Cesarean/Support Education and Concern), an organization of Cesarean couples whose goal is to inform, console, and educate other Cesarean couples. I wrote them a letter and was surprised at the personal, warm, and understanding reply I received. These people knew exactly how I felt and told me that under the circumstances, all my reactions to the Cesarean were normal.

Two events occurred shortly afterwards that had healing powers for my ailing mental state. First, I was asked to speak at a Lamaze childbirth class. My sensitive instructor, who had endured my ranting and raving for months and who had seen the Cesarean rate increase as high as 40 percent in some hospitals, thought perhaps that I could help prepare her current class for the possibility that all expectant mothers face. I spent lots of time sifting through the events and feelings relating to my pregnancy and childbirth experience. What therapy! After repeating my story out loud several times, I could for the first time laugh at myself.

Secondly, I attended a local C/SEC meeting and was again awed by the fact that so many other women had been just as determined as I to have natural childbirth and were certainly just as disappointed and traumatized to instead deliver by Cesarean. One woman there admitted she did not even want to take her baby home from the hospital. My anger and "why me?" attitude surrendered to compassion as I listened to other mothers describe my ordeal.

I left the meeting with stacks of leaflets and pamphlets full of hard-to-find Cesarean childbirth details. Also I discovered there are Cesarean childbirth classes available in some hospitals. A couple should be prepared and informed if they're going to share in the birth of their baby.

My hopes are soaring. My next Cesarean birth experience could be wonderful. It will definitely not be the disaster of my first one. I am planning to get pregnant next year. Everything will be great. I keep thinking about my husband and me in the operating room. I can see it all now. □

WHY WE CHOSE ARTIFICIAL INSEMINATION

By Saundra DeWitt

"To further complicate matters, I could no longer deny the existence of a strong urge for biological motherhood. I had always dreamed of being pregnant, giving birth, and nursing my baby."

When my husband and I weren't getting pregnant, the first course of action my gynecologist suggested was a sperm count. Steve and I greeted the results with disbelief. He *couldn't* be sterile! He was so healthy and virile, and none of the usual causes seemed to apply.

However, further testing confirmed Steve's condition, and we had to adjust to the painful fact we'd never have a baby of our own. After five years of marriage, we were "ripe" emotionally and financially to start a family. As the initial shock subsided, we resolved to take positive steps in that direction.

My doctor outlined the available options: A.I.D. (artificial insemination by a donor) or adoption. The idea of A.I.D. left us cold. It struck us as an unnatural and dehumanizing procedure. Besides, why bother with pregnancy and birth if the baby was still only half ours? It didn't seem right.

So we chose adoption. We felt we could be good and loving adoptive parents. We soon had the chance to prove it, for within months of applying to a private agency, we had the astounding luck to be offered a baby.

Suzanne was two months old. She had auburn hair and big blue eyes. It was love at first sight. I wept with tears of happiness and relief as I held our tiny new daughter. At long last, our dream was becoming a reality.

Soon afterwards we reapplied to adopt. We very much wanted a brother or sister for Suzie, and we knew the customary wait was four to six years. Secretly, we hoped to beat the odds again as we had with Suzie.

But by the time our daughter turned three years old, our hope had just about run out. A second baby was nowhere in sight, and we felt the need to reevaluate our position. Time was becoming our enemy, and we needed the answers to questions that only time would reveal.

For example, would we indeed be offered another baby for adoption? If so, how old would Suzie be? Would I feel like "starting all over again" if she were school-aged? And what about my own profession, which I looked forward to reentering?

Steve and I had definitely reached a crossroads of our own making. To further complicate matters, I could no longer deny the existence of a strong urge for biological motherhood. I had always dreamed of being pregnant, giving birth, and nursing my baby. I wasn't so sure I wanted another child through adoption.

If this realization was painful, the prospect of admitting it to Steve was even more so. In no way did I wish to add to his sense of "guilt" over our lack of biological parenthood. However, I knew nothing good would come from hiding my feelings.

As a result, we began earnestly discussing A.I.D. once more. Over the next few months, we each did some intensive soul-searching. At last Steve felt he could endorse the effort. That was good enough for me. It was as though a great weight had been lifted from our shoulders. We had nothing to lose and everything to gain by simultaneously pursuing both adoption and A.I.D. We felt recharged.

My gynecologist had me begin a basal body temperature record to establish my ovulatory pattern. He also performed a tubal insufflation, a simple procedure done in the office, to ensure that my fallopian tubes weren't blocked. Then he referred us to a fertility clinic.

At the clinic we obtained further leads, and after several inquiries, we chose a gynecologist in private practice. This doctor's warm, confident manner put us at ease, and his 100 percent success rate with A.I.D. was pretty convincing. Just the same, Steve and I were wary of becoming too optimistic.

Within two weeks our doctor had located a donor. We were elated. We did not learn the donor's identity, of course (nor he ours), but were given pertinent facts such as age, nationality, profession, physical characteristics, and health history. Our donor seemed like an excellent match to Steve in every respect.

On the basis of my temperature record, the doctor would perform one to three inseminations per month. Most of our doctor's A.I.D. patients conceived within four menstrual cycles. When Steve and I passed this "magic" number, we were quite disappointed. Actually, the tension each month just prior to the start of a new cycle was almost unbearable. By the time the seventh cycle had come and gone, we were duly concerned even if our doctor wasn't. My anxiety was such that I now required a mild tranquilizer during my fertile time. The strain also led Steve and me to contemplate a cutoff point. Whenever I felt really down, I'd wonder if we would become the first failure.

Fortunately, the passage of the eighth cycle was to change all that. For on the eighth attempt, we were blessed with the start of a healthy, full-term pregnancy. It's hard to imagine any couple being more thankful for the miracle of conception. Steve was immensely relieved, and as it turns out, he couldn't have been prouder of my swelling abdomen.

When I entered my sixth month, Steve and I enrolled in a prepared childbirth class. Probably the only difference between our pregnancy and others was this: when I'd try to picture who the baby would look like, I'd draw a blank.

It's as though I had mated with a ghost. I hoped the baby would resemble me, but I wasn't counting on it.

A week before my due date, my water broke. On the way to the hospital, Steve and I were quivering with excitement and fear—there was no turning back now. Steve proved to be a loving, dedicated coach during my ensuing 11-hour labor. Thanks to his steady presence, I was able to pass up all medication, as I had originally hoped.

At last the long-awaited moment arrived. With one final triumphant push, I introduced our son, Adam, to the world. Steve swore he heard trumpets go off. What he actually heard was our son's lusty cry. Steve proudly held our baby while my episiotomy was being stitched. As our doctor later commented, "There was some good old-fashioned bonding going on."

When nursing Adam (his time to be cuddly), I'm often overcome by his perfection. He's fulfilled all our needs, and then some. I can't imagine, and neither can Steve, that it took us nearly four years to decide on the matter. Were we to want more children, there would be absolutely *no* hesitation on our part to go the A.I.D. route.

We would also encourage anyone else in similar circumstances to try it. It's truly amazing how one positive pregnancy test can wipe away years of negative feelings and frustrations caused by the random whim of nature.

If cost is a consideration, it might be reassuring to know that A.I.D. compares favorably with adoption. In fact, in most instances it costs less. The usual charge for an insemination is $50. While most insurance policies don't cover this, they do pay for the resulting pregnancy and birth.

Steve and I will always feel doubly blessed to be both adoptive and "natural" parents. Both Suzie and Adam are ours to cherish. In addition, we have the satisfaction of knowing that A.I.D. has rounded out our family in the best way possible for us.   □

CHAPTER 2

EMOTIONAL HIGHS AND LOWS

CHASING THOSE BLUES AWAY

By Susan Flamholtz Trien

"The newness of our baby and the joy we felt in our accomplishment lifted me to a euphoria that kept me floating and gloating for our first weeks home. Then several unexpected things began to happen—or rather, not to happen."

Postpartum blues? Not me. I was too well prepared. My job as public relations writer for a childbirth education organization gave me tremendous insight into the events of pregnancy and childbirth. I had written countless educational materials for other expectant couples. Armed with facts and confidence, I was determined that I would have a smooth transition to motherhood.

I knew exactly the type of birth experience I wanted. My husband, Dave, and I were going to share in the culmination of the wondrous event we had planned and begun together. We had heard tales of how other fathers were ushered away from their wives at the crucial moment of delivery; how babies were whisked away from mothers immediately after birth to be brought out at four-hour intervals as if they were hospital property. We would have none of this.

We chose to enroll in the nurse-midwifery service at Roosevelt Hospital in New York City. Here, husband participation is the rule rather than the exception. Babies may stay in their mothers' rooms, and fathers—unrestricted by visiting hours—come to see their wives and cuddle their newborns any time they please.

At each of my prenatal checkups, I saw one of five nurse-midwives, all of whom were delighted when my husband chose to accompany me on several of my visits. I always brought along my little spiral notebook crammed with the myriad questions that cropped up in my mind between visits. There was always ample time for my concerns, and I felt that each midwife really cared about me as a person. When the spark of life inside me erupted into a tiny heartbeat, the midwife was as moved as I. "Tell your husband to come next visit," she urged excitedly. "Let's let him hear it too."

Although I had a very prolonged and exhausting labor, everything worked out as I envisioned it. My most vivid memory is of the strength and support Dave gave me. During transition, when I seemed to be drowning in the waves of my contractions, I clung tightly to his arms and stared into his eyes for reassurance. When I forgot how to breathe and began losing control, he breathed in unison and pressed the rhythm of the breathing pattern into my arms with his fingers. "This one can't last forever," he kept repeating. "You can do it. It's almost over." And just when I thought I couldn't handle it without medication, the midwife told Dave to hurry and change to his gown, and I felt that irresistible urge to push.

I'll never forget the exquisite joy I felt as my daughter lay, seconds old, in my arms. "Oh my God," I remember yelling. "I can't believe it! My beautiful daughter. My Stacey." Dave pulled down his mask and kissed me on the lips. Then I tried to breast-feed right there on the delivery table. The midwife asked if we'd like our picture taken. Dave handed her the camera we had brought along, and our first family gathering was immortalized on film.

The newness of our baby and the joy we felt in our accomplishment lifted me to a euphoria that kept me floating and gloating for our first weeks home. Then several unexpected things began to happen—or rather, not to happen.

First, and what seems in retrospect the most inconsequential problem, none of my clothes fit me. I had scrupulously stuck to a healthy diet and exercised regularly throughout my entire pregnancy and was certain I'd spring back into shape. When the baby was three weeks old, Dave and I decided to splurge and have a much-needed dinner out at our favorite restaurant. Wanting to look something like the woman he once knew, I rummaged through my closet for something special to wear. The only thing that fit was a pair of slacks I had bought when I was three months pregnant. Because my breasts were enlarged from nursing, none of my blouses could be buttoned, and I was forced to wear one of my smaller maternity tops. In addition, my inexperienced let-down reflex caused me to leak milk all over my clothes, and I had to wear bulky pads that added to my self-consciousness. By five weeks postpartum, things weren't much better: only two or three pairs of stretched-out old jeans could be pulled over my hips. I knew that it took at least six to eight weeks to gradually get back into shape—I had written it in brochures often enough. What I didn't know was how emotionally devastating it could be to wear maternity clothes for so many weeks after childbirth.

Our resumption of sexual relations was still another source of anxiety. I went for my four-week postpartum visit with the joyous expectations of a new bride. At long last my husband and I could regain some of the closeness I felt we were losing because of our intense involvement with the baby. We never seemed to have time to talk to each other anymore. I saw this rekindling of our physical intimacy as one way of picking up the threads of our former relationship. That night we made sure that the baby was sound asleep, had some drinks, turned on the stereo, and relaxed to some soothing music. While I had been told to "take it easy" on resuming relations, no one had prepared me for the degree of discomfort that I felt, and I burst into tears of disappointment and frustration. How long does this last? I wondered. Would anything in my life ever be the same?

But more overwhelming than anything else was the fatigue I felt during the first month and a half. Nursing the baby every two hours during the day and several times a night took its toll. With each nursing session lasting 30 to 40 minutes—that is, if the baby wasn't crying. Thus my day was broken into many tiny fragments of time. If I didn't nap to rejuvenate myself, my nerves were sure to snap. Any additional tasks, such as housecleaning or preparing for dinner guests, brought me to exhaustion and the brink of tears.

When, after the first month, I did begin to feel a little stronger, I was confronted by still another unexpected feeling—loneliness and isolation. As a working woman, my life had been, for the past eight years, city and job-based. My suburban apartment was a place to come home to, a retreat after a hard day's work. Suddenly, the sociological term "nuclear family" became a reality for me. When my husband arose and dressed and left for work, I felt as if I were abandoned on a barren island without a raft. My main event was walking down the aisles of the supermarket and, with a carriage to maneuver, even that was difficult. I was locked out of places by too many steps or signs bearing the words "No Baby Carriages." When my husband returned from work and changed for a quick game of tennis "with the boys," I felt even more bereft and overreacted with resentment. It seemed that I would never be free and that, even if I were, I was too tired to do anything but take a walk around the block and come home to collapse in a heap.

Happily, I am writing all of these things in retrospect, for, as I learned, the old adage, "Time heals all wounds," is especially true of the postpartum period. By the time the baby was two months old, I began to feel, look, and act the way I used to. (Not coincidentally, this was also around the time that the baby began to sleep through the night.)

As I felt better and went out more often, I began to see that a carriage can be like a magnet, attracting new friends who are in the same position. With my renewed strength I was able to resume some of my former outside interests while Dave watched the baby. Having my own outlets, I no longer resented my husband's freedom to pursue his interests. The baby herself was and continues to be an ever-increasing source of delight and fascination for both of us. Watching each new step she takes is like witnessing an exciting discovery.

It seems, then, that the best cure for the postpartum blues is a liberal dose of time—time for your body to go back into shape and to regain your physical strength; time for the baby to become adjusted to her life outside the womb and to develop a less demanding schedule; time to shift emotional gears and to develop new friends and interests. You can't rush any of these things; all are intertwined. You just need a little patience. □

CUTTING THE CORD

By Susan Mendonca

"Their growth will leave little scars on the fabric of my life, which will heal over, but I will always remember, and they will quickly forget."

As I enter the living room, I see Gabriel's dark head bobbing behind the reclining chair. He teeters on thick, muscular legs, his little toes splayed out to balance him precariously. His eyes meet mine, and a ready smile reveals two new teeth. He forgets to hold on; his plump body keels over with a decisive thud onto the carpet.

There is something irresistible about him. He is unlike his sister, who sits on the floor doing a puzzle, her security blanket swathed around her slender body making her look like a folded peapod.

Gabriel bounces with an aggressiveness that makes my arms ache to hold him. His hair makes long, airy wisps around his ears. He grasps my cheek with an iron grip and wrenches the skin when he laughs at my contorted face.

I place my son in the highchair, and he slaps the tray and shouts for me to hurry up with his lunch. And when I bring the food, there is that elastic smile again. He takes a piece of cheese and squelches it between pudgy fingers, rocking and chuckling simultaneously.

I have tried not to indulge in loving him too much yet. I feel a little guilty and very aware of the hot stare of two large blue eyes that burn mine with jealousy. I am torn between the two of them; my love for each of them is so different. I meet my daughter's gaze as if I have caught my own reflection in a clear puddle. I know what she feels. For Emily's sake, I restrain myself from abandoned displays of Oedipal affection.

But when she leaves, like a naughty child I scoop Gabriel into my arms and hold him close to me, my last baby, my only son. For I know in too few years he will join the ranks of men and a wall of sexuality will separate us, and only a hint of our original tie will underlie our relationship.

My husband, a physical education teacher, was so ecstatic that he purchased a baseball bat and glove for his newborn son. (He did the same thing when Emily was born, by the way.) And I know that my husband and the world won't allow Gabriel to be a baby for very long, and that knowledge stabs me and makes me cling to him fiercely, as if we were floating down a raging river.

I have watched my daughter these past months; Emily drifting away from me and joining the stream of kindergarten consciousness, like a fish who knows its time and joins the others automatically. She has made that adjustment fluidly, as if it needed no explanation. I mentioned once in a wistful moment, "I'll miss you when you're in school," and she didn't even look up from the collage of colored paper that was strewn like large confetti across the living room carpet. "You'll get used to it, Mommy," she told me matter-of-factly.

So, as Emily races down the front steps and enters the automatic, wheezing doors of the school bus, Gabriel remains on his hands and knees on the carpet. Losing sight of me for a moment, he suddenly feels a void. He lets out a shout, a howl, and then tears. It is as if we have been torn apart; he cannot fathom that separation; he cannot understand that I am only in the next room. I leave the laundry in a rumpled mound on the bedroom floor and go to him.

Gabriel scrambles over a group of pillows to reach my breast, tugging on it roughly before rooting. "You ought to give up nursing him. He's eight months old now; he could drink from a cup," people tell me. But we are happy this way. He nuzzles against me, and although his whole body doesn't fit on my lap anymore, I feel complete. It is the place where we connect.

When Emily comes home, her yellow slicker makes simultaneous puddles on the linoleum. She peels off her rubbers, leaving them by the back door like discarded skins. She curls up in front of the TV for a while, then seeks me out to give me an account of her day. She has collected wet, yellow leaves from the sidewalk in front of our house. She sits next to me. Her woolen sweater feels cold and prickly against my bare arm, a sharp contrast that slices us apart for a moment. Yet we blend together quickly.

She shows me the leaves, each one individually, and she is absorbed in their distinctive beauty. I admire them with her. She smiles at the leaves in her lap with that exquisite curiosity that belongs only to a child. Unknowingly, Emily draws me away from my adulthood so that I can share a moment of her magical childhood.

I want to remember this day. I want it pressed into my memory like dried flowers between the pages of a book. The wet streets, yellow leaves encircling the trees out front, spattered like dabs of paint along the sidewalk. The necklace of drool that is suspended from my breast to Gabriel's parted lips. And Emily's warm dampness pressed close to me.

I think of all the things my husband, in his dear exuberance, has planned for Gabriel the football quarterback "who eats like a champ" is already, at eight months of age, a champ in his father's eyes. A boy's manhood begins so painfully early. I wonder if it will hurt, or whether, as with Emily, it only hurts me. Their growth will leave little scars on the fabric of my life, which will heal over, but I will always remember, and they will quickly forget. Just as I have long forgotten those things that my mother cherishes as the landmarks of my growing up. And all that either Gabriel or Emily will ever say will be, "Don't worry, Mommy. You'll get used to it." And in some strange way, their words will be a comfort to me, and I will get used to it. □

LEARNING TO LOVE MY SECOND CHILD

By Diane Mordaunt Gulbas

*" I laid back, confused, overcome by ambivalent feelings of failure
and fear. That instant sense of devotion and protection that
I had counted on was absent."*

Poor little one. Ugly and still red from your birth three months ago, you
lie in your crib pleading for love, while I search for the right place in my
heart for you.

Squirming, grunting, flailing—you're so different from your sister. Even
your entry into this world was different. What had been an enjoyable, ethereal
pain before was agony with you. Unable to form a logical compromise between
the intense love I felt for my firstborn and the affection I knew you would
demand, I wept silently between contractions. Postpartum blues, the nurses
said. Postpartum? This was intrapartum. What was wrong with me?

Your arrival was precipitous. Two hours later and there you were, a 6 lb. 9
oz. boy, the complete antithesis of your sister. Bald and wrinkled, with a
smashed-in nose and small chin, you looked more like a newborn Pekingese pup
than a human. Even the pictures in the motherhood manuals hadn't looked like
you. Or so I thought. Deep inside I knew you were a normal-looking newborn,
but something was clouding my senses.

We had planned for you, had been joyous over the news that I was pregnant, and had watched with excited anticipation your development as my
stomach grew and rippled with your movements. Then why couldn't I hold
you when they placed you on my belly? Where was the bonding? Had the
supreme order of things collapsed so that the supposedly instinctual love was
missing, that instinct so basic to all animal species?

I handed you to your daddy, all decked out in his blue scrub suit. Even the
sight of father and son failed to evoke a response. I laid back, confused, overcome by ambivalent feelings of failure and fear. That instant sense of devotion
and protection that I had counted on was absent.

Afterwards they wheeled me to recovery. The pediatrician came in with
your exact dimensions and pronounced you healthy. I shut my eyes and waited
for the magic to begin, that intense emotional high that I had felt the first time.
But no magic came.

The next morning I gathered myself together, sucked in my stomach, and walked down to the nursery to see you. You were the smallest, reddest one in the group. My heart sank. I had thought maybe you had plumped up overnight, but you hadn't. I walked back to my room feeling guilty and confused, ignoring the happy family gatherings in the halls.

That afternoon your sister came to visit. Sixteen months older than you, she waddled around the halls laughing, her blue eyes shining. I showed her off to all the personnel, as if in reparation for my little reddened one in the nursery. I felt myself silently saying, "See what I'm capable of producing!" Hours later, as we were having our togetherness supper of steak and champagne, my husband gently reminded me that she had looked exactly like you at birth. I wouldn't accept his words. I remembered her as being beautiful and perfect from the start, and I just couldn't make the transition between you and my little blond angel.

Several days later it was homecoming time, and we had arranged for your sister to be elsewhere when we arrived with you. The books said this was a good way to forestall any jealous feelings on the part of the older sibling. When Amanda did come home with her grandmother, you were fast asleep in your bassinet. But not for long. "Baaaby!" she squealed, and with an eagerness surpassing my highest expectations, she ran to you, rocked the bassinet, and generally revelled in the delight of your presence. Certainly no jealous feelings here, I thought. Maybe later. Surely, she'll resent you later.

But she never did. She was gentle (as gentle as an energetic eighteen-month-old can be) and protective from the beginning. Actually, I never gave her reason to be jealous. Your demands were small, and I satisfied them with what modicum of time your physiologic limits dictated. You were fed, burped, and put back in the crib. Guilt feelings tugged stronger at my heart, and as you lay there, eyes wide, brow furrowed, I imagined your saying, "Look at me! I'm cute too! Please play with me." I began to hold you more, talk to you, and watch your smile develop, while I waited for the sense of my expanded family to engulf me, but my efforts were forced and artificial, with none of the spontaneity that I had felt before.

One afternoon I timidly voiced my concern to one of my friends. I was actually scared to bring it out in the open. Like admitting you beat your child or drink too much, saying you don't think you love your son is a difficult confession. To my surprise, she didn't react with the accusing horror I had anticipated. Quite the contrary, she acted as if this were a normal and natural feeling and that the only thing not normal and not natural about it is the reticence of mothers to talk about it.

"Everybody prepared you so well for the first," she said. "They assume you don't need any aid adjusting to the second. When, in fact, dealing with a second, especially a short-spaced second child, can be much more emotionally trying than the first."

I asked her if she had felt this way.

"Oh sure," she responded. "It wasn't until my son was eleven months old that I felt the real love. And that's when I learned the difference between dividing my love and doubling it."

"What happened?" I asked.

"It was something. I won't explain it to you now. But it will come to you. Just don't worry. You're not an inadequate mother. Merely a truthful one."

Her words were immensely reassuring. If only more of us would be open about our feelings, instead of hiding them behind rose-colored bunting, our feelings of inadequacy, insecurity, and guilt would be assuaged, and we could tune in to more positive emotions. I began to talk to more and more people about my "problem" and discovered that, though not universal, it was certainly a prevalent situation.

Meanwhile I wondered about the turning point my friend had mentioned. A developmental milestone? A religious experience? I didn't know, but I watched for it like a hawk.

Then, little one, your nose began to run. Clear, then yellow, crusting your nostrils and hampering your breathing. You grunted and snorted when you took the bottle. I turned the humidifier on and administered nose drops. That night I was fixing dinner when your daddy came in with you in his arms and said, "I think he's running a fever." That terrible wave of panic that only a mother with a sick child can appreciate swept over me. This is it, I thought. This is the turning point. But why illness? Why does he have to hurt, so that I can love?

That night, I stayed with you in the nursery, rocking you, cuddling you. We made up stories about the animals on the wallpaper, we sang, and we held literary critiques on every nursery rhyme in the book. Somewhere around 4 a.m. your daddy came in and said I was overreacting, that it was probably just a cold and nothing to worry about. I smiled. I wasn't overreacting, I was just beginning to react. I felt like a mother again.

Your doctor said that you had a respiratory infection, that you'd be fine, and he asked me why I was crying.

"Because I have two children and I love them both so much," I answered. He nodded as if he understood. He didn't, though.

But you and I do, don't we, little one?   □

THANKSGIVING BABY

By Judith Kamin

"No one really suspected my depression, my inadequacies. I didn't know who I had become. But whoever I was, I hated myself."

Last year I had a son. I loved him and hated him from the start. Mostly I felt guilty. Obsessively, I relived his birth. I was admitted to the labor room on an icy Tuesday at two o'clock in the morning in such a rush that I didn't even put stockings on. My legs, like my face, were mottled by the hostile Chicago wind. I paid no attention to that. What I really wanted was to be ten years old again riding my bicycle down the steep hill by the school playground, braids flying in the air; I would have settled for curling up tightly on the concrete floor.

Trembling, clammy with fear, I waited while the protocol of admission was carried out. It was all so mechanical, so impersonal, as secret as the rites of primitive tribes, structured and peculiar. The nurse, possessing a figure as lean as a ski pole, rang a buzzer situated directly to the left of two prisonlike steel doors.

"Should only be a moment. Sometimes seems to take longer though," Miss Crawford said, spearing me with her glance. "Have to do it this way so the babies keep safe."

This can't be happening, I thought. Not to me. If only it were as easy to have a baby as to talk about it. This was so humiliating; so lacking in all privacy.

Sudden footsteps dissected my thoughts. The doors swung open, and I was forced inside. I felt as though I were trapped in a corridor of snakes. All possibilities of escape were blocked.

"Will my husband be able to find me?"

"It looks like he already has," she chuckled, as Howard ambled down the hall. Nothing ever disturbs him, I thought resentfully. I'm always the one who has to suffer. Why doesn't fear spring into his eyes? Why doesn't his face turn pale like in all those romantic books I read? Why is he always so in control while I'm buffeted by a million anxieties and ambivalences? I wished that just once he'd feel the kind of self-pity that I experience. But he is so handsome; his hair beginning to gray, his mouth curving in sweetness.

"Would you like a taffy apple?" he teased.

"Howard," I whispered, in a voice I hardly recognized as my own. "I just heard something pop."

"Pop? Like Pop Goes the Weasel?"

I felt a kind of hysteria begin. Perhaps that warm fluid running down my legs was blood. My anxieties transmitted themselves to Howard for once. He sped into action. Then it all blurred. Everything raced like a film projector run backwards. All I ever remembered afterwards were isolated scenes: Dr. Sinclair with a big fat cigar in his mouth. I thought back to the first time I'd seen Dr. Sinclair right before Howard and I were married.

I sat in his waiting room hour after interminable hour, listening to doors opening and slamming in the inner office and nobody coming out. Finally, I was ushered into a room with that frightening clawlike table, which I tried mightily to avoid looking at. It seemed to me a bed of nails as I lowered myself upon it—a payment for sexuality. But he was nice to me. I thought he was handsome as a movie star. Now here he was bending over me.

"Would a movie star smoke a cigar?" I asked, drunk on Demerol.

I fought as my hands were strapped and my feet placed into those rat trap stirrups. Howard was gone. Dr. Sinclair looked sternly down at me. "I'm sorry," I said typically, and fell into an irresistible sleep in spite of my panic.

I awakened in a dark, high-ceilinged room to the news that I had a fine son, and then I was holding him while his father grinned. Both the baby and I were fuzzy.

"Oh, Howard, he has hair in his ears like you do and tiny, Gothic cheekbones."

My baby dazzled me. Only Howard and I could have produced this unique little human being. And he was beautiful, with a pixie haircut like mine, a miniature cleft in his chin, and slate blue eyes, which I hoped would turn into the changeable hazel that runs in our family. So Nicky was loved.

But I was also afraid for him. A kind of premonition of the days to come possessed me. How I longed to remain totally passive in this hospital. How I loved being taken care of.

And how I envied Nicky when I handed him back to the nurse. He could sleep, but I was alone with my forebodings, with my fear of responsibility. I wished we could have stayed together in the bubble of my body. I didn't want his separation. The numbered bracelets on our wrists were all that linked us. Like concentration camp tattoos. I really was so confused.

"Come home in four days instead of five," Howard said, "I miss you." Tears filled my eyes. "I don't want to go home!" I cried, pushing away from him and running to my room. He looked as startled as I felt.

The last night in the hospital came too soon. I gave Nicky to the nurse, and again I slept. For the last time.

The next morning we were escorted to the door of the hospital. Nicky was covered with a blanket to protect him from the shock of the air. "Baby boy, you be good to me and I'll be good to you," I intoned, but he stiffened in my arms and wailed.

And thus began the pattern of our days. When I was pregnant, taking care of the baby had meant taking care of myself. That was easy. Now I had Nicky to contend with. I existed from feeding to feeding. My brain was like a blueberry muffin. Nothing I did could satisfy him. He never slept, he only dozed. He demanded, then rejected me. His feedings became a nightmare. He took one or two ounces and spit them up, then screamed himself to sleep. It was all such a circle. When Nicky cried, I raged at Howard. He, in turn, yelled at his secretary. Whom did she turn to? I wondered.

How could one baby disrupt the world? I felt such a multiplicity of emptiness. I was too paralyzed to feel anything positive. "How's the baby?" all my friends would say. "Can he turn over yet?" No one asked about me. No one really suspected my depression, my inadequacies. I didn't know who I had become. But whoever I was, I hated myself. And I was angry with Nicky.

Mostly, though, I suppose I just felt guilty. Why couldn't I cope with this? I asked myself for the hundredth time as I lay awake shaking, waiting for Nicky to cry. Why did I wish him out of existence? How I wished I had never taken this giant step. And how I hated Howard when he talked about the "baby blues" with his all-knowing, smug smile. Yet later that night as I fed Nick, a tiny gas pain smile flitted like a butterfly wing across his face. "How lovely his smile will be," I breathed aloud. Then he wailed, and my trembling began again.

In those months after Nick's birth, I was constantly ashamed and too exhausted and involved with myself to even read the newspapers. I would tiptoe into his room, afraid even to breathe, look down into his crib, and wish I were an infant again and could sleep. I knew I was acting like a child, but I did not have the real advantages of being one. And I certainly had abdicated from the adult world.

"Judy, honey, can you manage to make dinner just one night a week?"

"No!" I screamed, "and neither could you if you were saddled with that baby all day."

"You're drowning in self-pity." Howard was exasperated though remarkably patient.

Christmas was coming. The thought of it was more than I could bear. I knew Nick and I were defeating each other. I was not meeting his needs. I was not adapting. One day, to celebrate Nick's three-week-birthday, Howard brought home a brightly painted carousel. We turned it on. "Love Makes the World Go Round," played on and on.

Nick opened his eyes wide; he didn't even startle. He listened as to a heartbeat, and the first real smile of his life illuminated his face. How intricate he is, I thought. How demanding. Perhaps he has been given to me to teach me how to love, to be less selfish, to consider his needs above my own frustrations. I had not done that before. I had made no effort to enter into his mind, to attune myself to him. I tried to imagine what he was thinking as he lay there surrounded by bumper pads and giants. Did he think? I didn't know, but I decided that if he could tell me, it would go something like this:

"Thank you for my wonderful carousel. It is so beautiful. I think it is the most beautiful carousel in the world. When I look at it, I feel so proud, and I don't mind anymore that I can't walk or talk. Every time I hear the music, I stop crying, and I feel happy. I love to watch the giraffe go round and round after the elephant and the donkey. You gave them to me, and as long as you and they are near, I need not be afraid. Why won't you be more patient with me, Mama?"

Standing in Nicky's room that snowy Sunday afternoon, I began to feel a real love grow. I had been fighting him. I began to feel that he and I were really part of one another; that he was at the beginning of life's cycle, that I was at the middle. In helping him to thrive, I could help myself. I played the game of entering into his mind often, and while I knew I was only projecting my own thoughts, I felt an empathy for him spring to life, a patience, a willingness to cooperate. I suppose all good mothers do this naturally, but I had to learn it. Nicky, with his marvelously responsive face and wiry body, did his part, too, in our mutuality. One day we walked in the park with our dog, Gulliver. Nicky really enjoyed these outings. His hands waved expressively about as if leading an orchestra. Perhaps if he could have spoken, this is what he would have said:

"Today I saw my first sunset. It was strange. And wonderful. I sat right next to Mama, and we watched it together. Afterwards she put me back in my buggy. It was very cold and bright out. I wanted to see everything. So I cried. And then she set me free. She carried me in her arms and tied the buggy to Gulliver. We walked that way all the way home. It was a swinging motion. I love to swing. Sometimes I fall asleep, and then I dream of warmth and people who will always love me."

When Nicky was four weeks old, on that snowy day in the park, I fell in love with him. My depression vanished; he slept through the night. Who knows what was the cause and what was effect or whether I communicated my new happiness to him? I only knew that I loved to hold him and take care of him and he truly was mine. I felt that we had all become a family, that we were as inextricably bound as the branches of a tree.

On my first afternoon out, with a generous neighbor baby-sitting, I took a taxi downtown. I asked the driver if he had any children.

"No, that's the one thing in life my wife and I want. How about you?" he replied.

I told him I had a son born at the end of November. He thought for a while, smiled through the rear view mirror, and stated with, was it envy? "Lady, take good care of him, he's your Thanksgiving baby."

It's a year later now. Nick is beginning to walk. The weather is vile, and we're forced to stay inside quite a lot. When I become irritated with Nicky's quest for new objects to touch and to put into his mouth, I think of the cab driver's words, and I give thanks. □

THE NEWNESS OF LIFE

By Carol Cyphers

"We have rededicated ourselves to live each day more fully, to appreciate and be aware of each other's special qualities, and to see our world and experience its beauty with all our senses."

"Life is really going to change when the baby comes." "How do you feel about starting all over?" were the comments I heard most when, at the age of thirty-six and almost ten years since my last child was born, I announced to friends and relatives that I was pregnant. Yet now when these same people see me with my infant daughter, Tara, the response is, "You must really appreciate this baby a lot more." I realize what they mean—not that I don't appreciate or love my other two children any less, but that with my added maturity and experience to guide me, I am savoring each moment with my little one for I know how quickly this time will pass.

When I was younger, I can remember thinking I would always have little children. Reaching my mid-thirties and having a teenage son and a daughter entering puberty seemed so remote to me. Now when I think about my son's going off to college in a few short years, I ask myself, "Where did all the years go?" Then I realize that they went one day at a time, just as they are doing now.

But something has changed. My mothering seems to have a better quality to it. At a time in my life when I am more involved than ever before in my own college education, my husband's business, my children's activities, and community projects, I am still able to make ample time to experience this baby to the fullest. I think what makes this possible is my attitude: toward mothering, toward organizing my time, toward the trials in life. I take more in stride, have a heightened awareness of my surroundings, and an ability to be more relaxed.

I've also learned to be flexible. It's always been important to me to have a clean house, but I've relaxed enough to know that moments spent with my family are worth sacrificing an immaculate home. Now it's all right if the laundry piles up for a day or the breakfast dishes sit in the sink until dinner. If Tara is having a fussy day and needs extra attention, everything waits while we sit and rock together.

My senses seem more alive too. I see, hear, touch, and smell things on a conscious level. When I hold Tara and nestle my lips in her neck as she molds her little body into a warm extension of me, I experience the sweetness of her baby scent, the softness of her hair, and the chubbiness of her skin. I listen to her giggle and tuck these moments safely in my memory for I know that it won't be very long before she will be squirming from my arms to investigate the neighbor's cat beneath a bush or running to catch a butterfly. Everything that is new to her becomes a new discovery for me. When I see Tara scoot a measuring cup along the floor and coo and sing as it rolls and delights her, I stop what I'm doing and sit down to watch the newness of her world. I don't take for granted her enthusiasm when she touches a puppy for the first time or feels the softness of a banana squishing between her fingers or smells its sweetness. I admire her determination to stand and then fall and try again. I try to see the world through her eyes.

The other day, for example, she crawled across the room, pulled herself up on the coffee table, and for the first time saw life from a different dimension. Even though the contents of the table were things she shouldn't touch, I knew what it must be like to see and not be able to touch. That would be like asking me not to dig my toes into the sand on my first visit to the beach. So unlike previous years, when I had spent so much time warning my toddlers not to touch Mommy's things, this time I baby-proofed the house by putting harmful objects completely out of reach and beyond temptation. Now we can both relax and enjoy the house. I know there's nothing that can really be broken or hurt her, and she can explore without someone constantly fussing at her.

Not only has my added awareness benefited Tara, but it has also reaped benefits for the whole family. It has been contagious. We seem to appreciate each other more. We watch and laugh and share Tara's new experiences and recall the memories of each of the other children. "What was the first word I said, Mom?" "When did I walk?" "Did you play with me that way when I was little?" they ask. Then the stories begin, and the family albums come out. Before we know it, the whole family room is strewn with pictures of each baby's first step and birthdays.

Tara has stimulated feelings that we had taken for granted. She has been a bright new beginning in our lives.

We have rededicated ourselves to live each day more fully, to appreciate each other's special qualities, and to see our world and experience its beauty with all our senses.

This beauty has been especially felt in the relationship between my husband and me. Many nights I have watched him standing silently beside Tara's crib and have often wondered what his thoughts were. But I don't wonder anymore. The other night when I heard his footsteps coming down the hall, then pause, I walked to the doorway of our room. I watched him take his special moments with the older children—a few words, a hug, a kiss. Then he walked into the baby's room and stood silently beside her crib with only his hand caressing her head. He turned toward me. With tears in his eyes and a voice almost inaudible, he gently took me in his arms and started to speak. "When I look at her..." his voice faltered. He held me even closer. I, too, had so much to say, but the only words I could speak were, "I know." □

THE TRAGEDY OF CRIB DEATH

By Patricia Hermes

"Although we put away the infant seat, the cradle, and the clothes, the empty spaces where those things had been seemed to speak silently of our loss."

Only the moonlight illuminated the room when my three-week-old daughter, Mary Beth, awoke, lustily announcing time for her 2 a.m. feeding. I reached out to the cradle where she slept alongside my bed and rocked her gently.

Mary Beth had been christened earlier that day. Surrounded by family and friends, she had been admired and held. Her grandparents in particular had been thrilled. Although they delighted in their two older grandsons, they found a special wonder in this first granddaughter. Now, however, at two in the morning, with the ceremony over and the house empty of guests, I was tired. Being the mother of three children was a big task, and I begged Mary Beth then for a few more minutes of sleep. She grunted a little, and then with a sigh, she slept.

When I awoke next, the sun was pouring through the windows of the bedroom. I could hear the boys stirring in their adjoining room, and I nudged my husband softly. "Matt," I whispered. "Mary Beth slept all night last night—the first time!"

Matt smiled and we snuggled sleepily, congratulating ourselves and our tiny daughter that a milestone had been reached. After a few minutes, Matt got up, tiptoed to the cradle, and reached down to touch her. But with that touch, our miracle ended and a nightmare began. Mary Beth was dead, the victim of a disease known since antiquity and as unpreventable now as it was then. The disease was Sudden Infant Death Syndrome (SIDS), also known as "crib death."

"Honey!" Matt said to me then, and his voice was so choked that I was immediately out of bed and standing beside him at the cradle. "Something's wrong with the baby!"

As Matt picked her up, she looked peaceful, as though she were still sleeping, but she lay in his arms terribly still. And although we covered her with blankets, we were not able to warm her tiny body.

At that moment—although we knew it was useless—we also knew we had to do *something*. Matt began mouth-to-mouth resuscitation, while I tried frantically to reach the pediatrician on the telephone.

"Mrs. Hermes?" he questioned me incredulously when the answering service put me through. "Your baby is dead?"

"I think so," I replied, crying. (I *knew* so, and I don't know why I said that.)

"This is what I want you to do," he said then, speaking very slowly and quietly. "I want you to bring her to the hospital."

"It won't do any good!" I sobbed.

"I know," he said, still speaking slowly, but now the authority in his voice reached me, and I was willing to stop thinking and do whatever I was told. "Just do it anyway. Bring her to the hospital right now. Do you understand?"

I didn't then, but I do now. Our pediatrician suspected immediately—and it was borne out later that day at the autopsy—that our daughter was a victim of Sudden Infant Death Syndrome. But being an experienced pediatrician, he also knew of the trauma, the police questioning and sometimes the suspicion of child abuse that often follows such a death. By having us bring Mary Beth to the hospital ourselves, he was able to say that she died there. Had we called the police or an ambulance that morning, they would not have been allowed to move her until a medical examiner had been summoned and an inquiry made. Our physician was trying to save us from that ordeal.

But although we were never questioned by the police, neither our pediatrician nor anyone else was able to shield us from what happened later. Our family and friends, although having heard of crib death, still found it impossible to believe that the healthy baby they had held in their arms the day before, was dead. It was too difficult to absorb the fact that yesterday they were at her christening; today we were summoning them to her funeral. Surely, we, her parents, had done something wrong, missed something, perhaps some sign of illness? Suspicion that I could have done something more, comments like, "If you had only..." caused guilt in me that was almost unbearable.

Even the most well-meaning remarks from family and friends hurt terribly. I remember my sister's saying that morning, "Wasn't there *something* you could have done?" And at the funeral my mother stood beside the grave and sobbed, "If you had only gotten up when she cried!" My pediatrician had already told both of us that that would not have made any difference. Death from SIDS, he told me, was instant. It could not have been prevented even if I had been holding her in my arms. In fact, he pointed out, the autopsy showed that Mary Beth had died, not at 2 a.m. but at about 6 a.m. "Had you fed her at 2:00," he said, "she still would have died at 6:00." But my mother found that as hard to believe as I did.

Sudden Infant Death Syndrome is the sudden and unexpected death of an apparently previously healthy infant, for whom at autopsy no adequate cause of death can be found. However, SIDS is not some random, unexplained phenomenon but an identifiable disease. At autopsy certain minute changes are found in the body that positively identify the child as an SIDS victim. Unfortunately, because these changes are only identifiable at autopsy, the disease remains unpredictable and, to date, unpreventable.

Because of this, it causes enormous trauma and often guilt in the families of its victims. Reactions of the police, and even family and friends, add to the grief and guilt that the parents already feel. In my own case, although the questions from my family hurt terribly, still I knew they loved and supported me in my grief. The reaction from the community showed no such support.

In the days and weeks following Mary Beth's death, no one in the neighborhood asked if I had hurt or neglected my child. But the most amazing and awful things happened. People who once spoke to me, who said "Good Morning" and "How are you?" avoided me now and would sometimes cross the street when they saw me coming. And although I knew that it was probably because they didn't know what to say, still it hurt that they wouldn't say anything. One morning I saw several friends of mine standing at the corner talking. They had their babies alongside them in strollers or crawling around on the grass. When I walked over to speak to them, each woman picked up her child and held it close to her. How my arms ached to hold a baby—any baby.

I began to wonder if there was something wrong with me. Was I becoming paranoid—suspecting slights and insults when, in fact, there were none? Or worse, did these people really think I had hurt my own baby, that I would somehow harm theirs? And the final, most terrible thought was the one I had many times in those days; that perhaps I *had* done something wrong. Should I have picked up Mary Beth when she cried? Wasn't there something I could have done? How could the doctor be so sure that she would have died anyway?

Whether real or imagined, the situation in the neighborhood soon became intolerable for both my husband and me. One neighbor, a particularly close friend, had had a son the same day as our Mary Beth was born, and this friend did not turn away from me. But now, watching David grow, watching him learn to sit up, to turn over, was a constant reminder. I would look at him and wonder silently: what would Mary Beth look like now? Would she be sitting up too? Would she be learning to crawl? Would this be the day she would first smile? Although we put away the infant seat, the cradle, and the clothes,the empty spaces where those things had been seemed to speak silently of our loss.

Within a few months we moved. The change of surroundings did help. In our new neighborhood no one knew about the baby, and I felt I could begin life again. But I didn't count then on what would happen inside of me. One cannot put away such an experience—pretend a child has never lived, never died—without paying an awful, internal price.

Fortunately, help was available to us, and although some of it was late in coming, we made use of it. For a time some personal counseling helped a lot. I was able to sort out what was real and what wasn't, what had to be accepted as truth, and what was not the truth—and the guilt was not the truth. And then, perhaps the best thing that ever happened to both my husband and me, we discovered an organization specifically founded to help the families of SIDS victims—the National Sudden Infant Death Syndrome Foundation. And we found it by accident through an announcement in a local newspaper.

Originally chartered as the Mark Addison Roe Foundation, in memory of an infant who had succumbed to the disease, the SIDS Foundation has chapters nationwide. The purpose of the organization is to spread understanding about the disease and to offer support and encouragement to parents who have to cope with this trauma. I don't think I'm exaggerating when I say this group was a lifesaver. When I met other parents who had gone through the same thing, when I heard them share feelings that I had had—feelings that were so awful when I thought I was alone with them—I began to feel for the first time that maybe I was going to survive intact.

The fact of my daughter's death I was able to accept. It was the details that hurt so much, that needed to be talked about. It wasn't until I had met another mother who had lost a child to this disease that I was able to talk about something that had haunted me for a long time. On the way to the hospital with Mary Beth the morning of her death, Matt drove the car and I sat alongside him. But I was not able to hold my daughter's body—she lay on the seat between us. For a long time I had felt guilty about that. Why wasn't I strong enough? If I was a really good mother, wouldn't I have held her in my arms? It was only after talking to other mothers that I began to feel that I wasn't abnormal or crazy. It wasn't that other mothers had necessarily felt the same way—some did, some didn't. It was just that the reaction was accepted as one of the many strange and sad things that can surround such a death.

Besides the SIDS Foundation, several other things happened in the succeeding years that made our lives return to the normal and happy lives we had had before. We had other children after Mary Beth's death. These children were not, and never will be, substitutes for the baby that we lost. Mary Beth lived. She had a place in our lives. She died. She will always be remembered and missed. But it was and is wonderful to have and hold each of our other children.

Finally, through all these years, the SIDS organization continues to be the greatest help. Although I do not feel I need to *receive* support so much anymore, I need to be able to give that support. I suppose I feel it gives some meaning to Mary Beth's life to know that if I can be of some help to others, then she did not live in vain. Today when I hear the mother of a recent SIDS victim say, "I feel as if I can't go on day to day," I think I understand something about how she feels. And although no one can truly know another's feelings, I can tell her that I remember a similar feeling.

It would be untrue to say that I have gotten over Mary Beth's death. I don't think anyone gets over such a thing. But one does get *better*. A friend of mine, herself the mother of an SIDS victim, once put it this way: "It's sort of like the shape of your heart changes. It will never be the same, because the baby is gone. But it does heal."

And it does heal—with time. But until researchers come up with an answer to this disease, groups like the National SIDS Foundation will be called upon to offer the healing that comes with time but can be hastened, and was hastened for me, with understanding and love. □

THOSE OLD POSTPARTUM, DAYTIME TV BLUES

By Suanne Smythe

"Like all new mothers, I was physically tired, and it was just so easy to flop down in front of the TV set while the baby slept or while I nursed him."

We read a lot today about what television is doing to the minds of our preschoolers and adolescents, but what about the damage it can do to the adult mind, particularly the young female adult mind trying to adjust to new motherhood?

As a working woman, I never had the opportunity to familiarize myself with the delights and dilemmas of daytime television until I had my first child and began staying home full-time to take care of him. I quickly discovered the companionship and tantalizing distraction the tube can offer. I wasn't exactly a stranger to the pitfalls of heavy TV viewing since my master's degree thesis had concerned its effects on adolescents. I was well aware of its escapist, violent, and anxiety-producing elements. Yet in spite of all that, I fell smack into the trap of "those old postpartum, daytime TV blues."

Like all new mothers, I was physically tired, and it was just so easy to flop down in front of the TV set while the baby slept or while I nursed him. Watching all the action on the game shows where "real folks just like me" were winning lots of prizes and big money, satisfied and depressed me at the same time. They made me feel as though *I* was doing something, *accomplishing* something, when, in fact, I was just becoming a video voyeur.

The commercials were no help either. I found myself scanning the kitchen *behind* the lady with the mop in the foreground to look for some clutter, some sign of disarray in her life. All those kitchens in TV commercials are so spotless, so squeaky clean, and mine was such a mess! When did I have time to polish chrome and admire my reflection? When could I scrub the floor until it was clean enough for my baby to eat off of? When could I polish windows until they seemed transparent? I had to sterilize bottles, watch TV, wash dirty diapers, watch TV, start dinner, and of course, watch TV.

Now we come to the "heart" of the matter—the soap operas. I found both positive and negative aspects in this viewing experience too. Here were people I could cope with, people I could understand (more or less), and people I could depend on to appear in my house during certain time slots each day.

Of course, the babies in the ads are generally beautiful and well-behaved, and children in soap operas seem to be off-camera most of the time—either asleep or being cared for by housekeepers—until they reach adolescence and can get into all sorts of trouble that might interest the viewing audience. By contrast, my own baby is "on camera" in my life constantly, and although much-loved, he is not always immaculate and grinning from ear to ear.

I found lots of food for the wrong kind of thought in the soaps. All the women are perfectly groomed and have gorgeous wardrobes, exciting careers, and adorable babies. Their homes are always neat and tidy, and they seem to make time for creative hobbies—painting, needlepoint, music—while still finding ways to care knowledgeably for their families and dispense advice to everybody in sight. And they all *talk* to each other so much! They're always getting dressed up to go out for dinner or lunch to hold long, intimate conversations over candlelit tables with gourmet meals they didn't have to prepare.

In contrast, my own postpartum existence seemed to consist of eating meatloaf on TV trays after the baby was asleep and talking with my husband during the commercial breaks about how we were going to pay our bills or cure our son's diaper rash. In short, everyone on the daytime serials was glamorous, competent, and free, while I felt dowdy, inferior, bored, and tied down. There seemed to be so much *action* on these dramas and so little in my life. I was used to being in an office all day, interacting with my co-workers, and I was lonely. There's only so much you can really say to a six-week-old, and as much as I hate to confess this, I found myself actually talking to the television set, telling the soap opera populace all those secrets they try to keep hidden from each other. The viewer can live vicariously through the soaps to a certain point, and then she can't help developing dissatisfaction with her own life, which involves a lot of mundane, routine activity—particularly in the case of a new mother.

The crisis-oriented nature of the daytime serials didn't help to lower my anxiety level, either. Each time one of the TV kids developed some disease, I found myself looking for similar symptoms in my own child, and when a premature baby on one of the soaps died, my empathy went far beyond the boundaries of what should have been my normal reaction.

But I'll say one thing for daytime TV shows—they did give my day some sense of order. After having worked at a career for so long, I found it hard to structure my days without an "agenda," and babies are not noted for their adherence to mothers' agendas. With so much "free time," I just couldn't seem to get *organized*. Daytime TV gave me a way to plan my days, i.e., "I'll make the beds and do the dishes before *The Mike Douglas Show* comes on, feed the baby and put him down for his nap between *Ryan's Hope* and *The Doctors,* and fold the clothes while I watch reruns of *The Dick Van Dyke Show*."

What had happened to my plans to take the baby out for afternoon walks, work at my free-lance writing while he napped, plan menus while he cooed in his playpen? What about inviting friends over or getting acquainted with the neighbors I hardly knew?

I think a number of elements came together in my life at once, leading to the dependency I formed on daytime television, and I'm sure I am not an isolated case. To begin with, our generation is the first one to really grow up with television. I can just barely remember when my family bought its first TV set. I was a preschooler at the time, so that means when I was a baby, my mother didn't have a television as an ever-present source of stimulation and education. This fact surely must have caused some difference between her infant-care practices and mine. She was forced to seek outside *human* help and companionship, and she undoubtedly had a more realistic view of motherhood than I did at the time my firstborn arrived. It's partly due, I think, to our mobile society, which causes families to become more isolated from each other, and partly due to the media hype we are exposed to day after day, showing us how new mothers should feel, how their babies should look, and most importantly, what new parents should *buy* for their offspring. In my case all of these things, added to my physical and emotional letdown following the birth of my child, combined to make daytime TV a very "easy way out" for me. This resulted ultimately in dissatisfaction, at least partial inertia, and a period of postpartum depression that lasted longer than it should have.

There are certainly many positive aspects about television, daytime and otherwise, that can provide beneficial relaxation, entertainment, and information, but perhaps some of the concern we feel about the programs our children are watching should spill over into adult viewing habits as well, particularly those of the vulnerable new mother.

I wish I could tell you that fate stepped in and I was saved when lightning struck our television set, and that after four days of agonizing withdrawal, I finally got my head on straight. But that would make a more suitable plot for TV than reality. Actually, one bright, sunny day, I caught myself sitting with the baby in my arms watching TV when I should have been outside getting some fresh air for both of us, and I decided then to cut back on my daytime TV habit. I took a look at the schedule, chose the programs I really enjoyed the most, and began turning the set off at other times during the day so I wouldn't be lured back to my old pattern.

Now I find myself branching out into new activities, getting out of the house more, enjoying my baby to the fullest, and generally feeling better mentally than I have in months. And I have made a solemn vow to avoid any relapse into "those old postpartum, daytime TV blues." □

WHO'S AFRAID OF A SEVEN-POUNDER?

By Richard Duquin

"I don't know what I had expected to see. What I did *see was what I thought had to be the smallest, ugliest baby in the world."*

"**Y**our wife asked me to tell you that Christopher is finally here. Congratulations," the doctor said as he walked into the father's waiting room and shook my hand. A short time later, I was on my way to the recovery room to see my wife and my new son.

I don't know what I had expected to see. What I *did* see was what I thought had to be the smallest, ugliest baby in the world. He was red and scrawny with a mass of black hair on his head that stood straight up. My wife was excited but tired after a long labor and delivery, and I was relieved when a nurse finally asked me to leave.

It was a long drive home. I thought about the baby lying in his little glass crib with wheels. I thought about my wife when they rolled her out of the labor room and into delivery. I remembered that lost, empty feeling as I walked alone to the father's waiting room. Suddenly I was angry with the doctor and with the hospital. If they had only allowed me to stay with my wife in the delivery room, then maybe I wouldn't have been so repulsed at the sight of my son. If I had seen him being born, if I had shared with him the moment he came into this world, maybe then I would have seen some beauty in the wretched little lump of skin and hair. Then, just maybe, I could have shared some of the joy that crept through my wife's exhaustion. At home I pushed all ugly thoughts from my mind, pulled out the list of names that my wife had so carefully prepared, and began to call relatives and friends to announce the arrival of our "beautiful" baby boy.

The next day at the hospital, my wife and I walked down to the nursery to see Christopher. Through the big glass window, he looked a little bit better, but not much, and he was still so very small. The hospital permitted the father to stay in the mother's room when the baby was brought in to be fed, but I was definitely not interested. I stayed with my wife until about 15 minutes before the baby was to be brought in, and I made up some wild excuse about why I had to leave. The following day I brought my mother to the hospital with me. Since she was there, we had to leave when the baby was brought into the room. On the third day I had invented another excuse as to why I couldn't possibly stay, but the hospital ruined my escape by bringing in the baby early.

The baby was not quite as red anymore, but he was still ugly—no chin, fat cheeks, and all of that black hair sticking straight up. The more I looked at him, the more I thought he looked like a chipmunk. Luckily for me, my wife had decided to breast-feed him. I didn't want to touch him, much less stick a bottle in his mouth. I think he knew how I felt since he obligingly fell asleep after eating, which gave me an airtight excuse for not holding him. ("We wouldn't want to disturb him now, dear. He looks so peaceful lying there.")

By the next day I didn't mind being in the same room with him. It was easier than trying to dream up excuses for leaving, and it was rather interesting to look at him. I still did not want to touch him, however. I watched my wife feed him. She seemed so gentle with him, so relaxed, so natural. But after he had finished eating, I noticed a tense tiredness in her face.

"What's wrong?" I asked.

She breathed a long sigh and replied, "I'm so tired. I'd just like to lie on my stomach for a while."

Now that could be a problem. If she was going to lie on her stomach, how could she hold the baby? The solution came to me like a thunderbolt.

"I'll call the nurse and have him taken back to the nursery," I announced gallantly.

"No," she blurted out. "You can't. They'd think I was a bad mother." Then she sighed again.

What could I do? She really did look tired, and I felt so guilty. At this point I really didn't have a choice.

"Give him to me. I'll hold him. You try to get some sleep."

Relief flooded her face, and she mumbled something about how the nurse would probably come soon. Then, she rolled over and closed her eyes.

For the next ten minutes, I sat very still, holding the little blue bundle. He lay there—not crying, but not sleeping either. His eyes seemed to be fixed on my face. I felt clumsy and big. My hands were huge next to his head. I thought about my father. He had always said that he wouldn't have anything to do with little babies until they were old enough to do something for themselves. "Too small," he always said. I remembered promising my wife that I wouldn't be like that. Then my mind shifted to all of the childbirth classes we had attended and how excited we had been. I thought about how confident I had been on the day we left for the hospital. I thought about how I had been a teacher for seven years and how I had always prided myself on my ability to handle kids. "You're afraid of him," I said to myself. It wasn't an earth-shattering revelation. I had known it all along, but admitting it gave me courage.

Carefully, I unwrapped his blanket and inspected his feet, ankles, and legs. He still looked very small, but oddly enough, his smallness had become fascinating. I held his hand and opened his clenched fist. He latched on to my finger.

"Pretty strong grip for a little guy," I said to him. I had actually said something to the little blue bundle. I felt silly. I looked up quickly to see if my wife had heard me. She hadn't. She was sleeping. I looked down. There he was, still awake, still looking in my direction.

"I must be doing something right," I muttered. "Well, little buddy, we've been sitting here for 15 minutes now. Maybe they'll come and get you soon."

That was how it began. For the next 15 minutes, I talked to him. I told him about Chaucer, our dog. I told him about baseball, football, and hockey. I told him that my students at school didn't pay attention to me as well as he did, and I promised him that when he got bigger, he could come to school with me for a day.

Then the nurse came.

"Getting acquainted with your son?" she asked.

I felt my face turn red as I nodded in response to her question. Then she took him out of my arms, put him in his little glass crib, and rolled him away. I looked over at my wife. She was still sleeping, so I left her a note and drove home. For the first time, I felt all of the proud, happy feelings that new fathers are always portrayed as feeling.

The next day when they came home, I carried Christopher into the house. I changed the first diaper (with some technical advice from my wife). I held him. I talked to him. I put him to bed.

As time passed, Christopher lost that newborn look. His arms and legs filled out. He developed a chin and his hair now lies flat on his head, except for a few curls. He smiles now, and when I talk to him, he talks back to me in the most intelligent gibberish I've ever heard.

When Christopher was three months old, my wife and I celebrated our third wedding anniversary. Over dinner in a small romantic restaurant, I admitted to her that I had been afraid of Christopher in the beginning.

"I was scared too," she said, "but I didn't have a choice. The nurses gave him to me, and I had to hold him and feed him."

So she had been afraid too. I thought about that for days. She had been afraid that the baby would cry and that she wouldn't be able to calm him. She had been afraid that she wouldn't know how to take care of him properly. All this fear had even made her afraid that maybe she didn't love him.

The more I thought, the more I began to wonder if my wife had just pretended to be tired that night. Had she recognized my fears because she had fears of her own? I never asked her, and I probably never will. I'd like to think that it was fate that brought Christopher and me together that last night in the hospital, but something deep down inside tells me that my wonderful wife gave fate a little push. □

CHAPTER 3

TO WORK
OR NOT
TO WORK

A NEW CAREER

By Lizabeth A. Snider

"I was counting my losses at not having time to devote to a teaching career, when, in fact, I had my most challenging teaching opportunity right at my fingertips."

It had been one of those dreary winter days, the kind that made me feel like the house was closing in on me. David would be working late, so I bundled Becky in her snowsuit and headed for the shopping mall. Walking through the high-ceiling corridors somehow helped to lift my spirits on such days, and Becky always squealed with excitement at the splashing fountains and hurrying shoppers. It had been this very place where David and I walked to pass the time when I realized I was in early labor. A year had slipped by since then, but the winter weather had coaxed me back to this enclosed springtime environment. I remembered that on the night Becky was born, it had been a soothing place to wait until it was time to leave for the hospital. As I pushed the stroller past the center mall exhibits, I caught my reflection in the huge department store window across the walkway. My physical appearance was considerably different now, but inside I was still waiting. In the past year I had come to develop an attitude of waiting patiently for time to pass, like a prisoner counting the days until the end of her sentence.

In the beginning the confinement had been unbearable, but soon I learned to bide my time creatively. I began sewing for Becky and doing needlework. I even took up baking bread and decoupage. I had been catapulted into a whole new lifestyle and was discovering what a major adjustment it was to change from a professional woman to a homemaker. Before Becky joined our family, David and I had been a career couple. I wasn't a corporate executive or a prestigious businesswoman, but my teaching was important to me. It was my talent, and I derived tremendous satisfaction from being successful at it. I had worked with handicapped children, and I took pride in my job to the point of feeling indispensable to those I taught.

All that was behind me now, though. I knew I could go back someday when Becky was older, but David and I had agreed that small children needed a mother at home, especially during the first two years. So when I learned I was pregnant, I gave up my teaching position and entered what I considered to be the limbo years. I resigned myself to the fact that the wait would be a long one. I would pass through that time as best I could until I was able to return to my work. I loved my baby, of course, and I loved being a mother. But really, straining cooked carrots and folding diapers could never be high points in my day.

I turned the stroller down another corridor. The pet shop was at the end of this one, and Becky was especially fascinated by the tropical birds that paced along their perches like wind-up toys. Just then a voice from behind called my name, and as I turned around I saw Anne coming toward me—almost in a trot. Even at a distance, one could get caught by her bubbling exuberance, and I found myself chuckling at the sight of her small form dancing through the dense crowd of shoppers.

"What are you two doing out on a day like this?" she asked. "You'd better get home before it starts raining."

"Needed a change of scenery," I sighed. "The pet shop was the best I could come up with on a day like today. How's school?"

"Hectic. You know how the kids get when they can't go outside. I just left my room as it was today and stopped by here on my way home. I've got my own crew waiting there. This is my own little 20-minute break between groups."

"I see your dilemma," I chuckled. Anne had six children of her own and a classroom of 20 more to whom she was equally devoted. Now *there* was a study in perpetual energy.

"Good heavens—look how this baby has grown. I can't believe it's been a year." She picked up Becky, giving her a little bounce in the air, and Becky responded with delight.

"I'll bet you're having a good time with her," Anne said, giving Becky another little bounce. "I just love it when they start their own little pattern of communication with you like this. I've never seen a baby's eyes sparkle so. You two must have some treasured secrets between you. I really miss my own children's being babies. Each one was so different, you know. I think it's God's greatest miracle to make each baby's personality so special. Well, I hate to run off," she said as she handed Becky back to me, "but I still have a few stops to make before I get home. Come see me!" she called as she disappeared into the crowd.

Her words hit me like a thunderbolt. Had I been oblivious to the thousands of special moments this child had been offering me for so many months? I looked at Becky, and she hugged me affectionately as if by some miracle she could know what I was thinking. I had spent a year of my life, and worst of all Becky's life, feeling inconvenienced at having to be the mother of an infant. Instead of basking in the joy of being the single most important person in her early life and seizing the opportunities that position offered, I had spent my quiet moments speculating on the future. I was counting my losses at not having time to devote to a teaching career, when, in fact, I had my most challenging teaching opportunity right at my fingertips. At that moment I became instantly aware of my role as the mother of this special infant. And things began to change for me, on the inside.

Now I approach each day with my daughter from a new perspective. I have put one career aside and launched another, just as meaningful and requiring a new kind of expertise. Just as I worked at becoming a successful teacher, becoming a successful parent also requires effort and dedication to a goal. Being a parent is not only a privilege but a very special challenge. Meeting that challenge brings innumerable rewards and an inner satisfaction that lasts a lifetime. I draw a salary of magic moments with my little one and a host of fringe benefits in hugs, kisses, and twinkling eyes.

Becky and I still do many of the same things. We stroll through the mall and make little excursions to our favorite spots around town. The difference is that we go together now. She is no longer just my bundle to carry, but she's my companion in countless special moments each day that we share with one another. I still strain carrots and fold diapers; every job has its drawbacks. And I haven't given up daydreaming about the future, either. But for the present, I am letting myself grow with my child while clocking in the hours of the most uniquely rewarding job ever—motherhood. □

JUST A HOUSEWIFE

By Donna S. Whitney

*"I realized that what I needed was to discuss my current job,
mothering, without feeling that I was a total bore.
I needed some peers in my profession."*

"**D**amn it, Jenny!" Our houses were only a driveway apart, and Mary's voice carried easily into my kitchen window, where I stood at the sink. Behind me my six-month-old daughter played happily with her toys. On the counter bread was rising. Soon we would go up to the den, where I was working on a quilt for a pregnant friend.

I felt contented and smug. I thought I had motherhood under control. My daughter slept through the night, and she took a morning and afternoon nap. I had been away from my job as a rehabilitation counselor with a caseload of 250 clients only since my daughter had been born, so I still savored my escape from that overwhelming responsibility. Now I only had one pair of hands plucking at my legs, a caseload of one for which I was just beginning to feel competent.

I did not understand my neighbor. Much of the time she cursed and complained about being bored. Being a mother was getting to her, she said. Just wait until my daughter was eighteen months old, she warned, but I decided I would do things differently.

I was the kind of mother I always thought I would be, at least hoped I would be. I had lost the weight I had gained during my pregnancy and then some. I breast-fed my daughter serenely and basked in the compliments about her beauty and health. I caught up on my correspondence with friends. I made my own baby food, baked bread, made jam, and experimented with recipes for interesting dinners.

I set myself apart from the other women in the neighborhood. It was not that I tried to avoid them but rather that I had made no effort to break into the routines they had established while I was still a working woman. I would see them gathered on someone's porch watching the children play, and I would stay inside. It wasn't shyness that kept me away but the fear of becoming one of the "housewives." Their lives seemed petty and boring. They probably watched soap operas all day and gossiped about each other. It seemed that their egos had become tied to their homes, their children, or their husbands. They often seemed angry, snapping at ther children. I felt different from, and yes, better than, these women. And up to this point I hadn't needed them.

But sometime around my daughter's six-month birthday, I began to wonder if she and I were incompatible. I wondered this secretly to myself because there was no one to discuss it with. I was uncomfortable about how aggressive she seemed, crawling over to other children and taking their toys. And since she had learned to stand up in her car seat (in spite of her seat belt), every car trip was a contest of wills.

I wasn't very happy about the person I was becoming. I began to yell at my daughter, and discipline was emerging as a touchy issue between my husband and me. Along with the developmental changes in my child and the resulting changes in our relationship came my realization that having a baby was for keeps.

I began to feel very alone with all these heavy thoughts. I felt my privacy infringed upon. Not only did I have very little time to pursue my own interests, but also being without a paying job left me with all the chores around the house. Face it, I thought, you're a housewife. The quilt I had begun as a loving gift now seemed an endless chore designed to keep me from intellectual pursuits. Breast-feeding was limiting me. Working mothers intrigued and threatened me.

Meanwhile, back at the office, rumor had it that I was doing just great and had really taken to motherhood. And I didn't want to tell them any different. Most of it was true, but there was no one with whom I could discuss my ambivalent feelings.

Naturally I thought about going back to work, mostly to regain my old status. But in spite of my problems with motherhood, I wanted to be the one to raise my child. Going back to work seemed too large a price to pay for ego-soothing. Who respected a mother? The only one who possibly could was another mother. I realized that what I really needed was to discuss my current job, mothering, without feeling that I was a total bore. I needed some peers in my profession.

I wasn't just going to walk out to the playground one day and start a heavy discussion about mothering. But I had recently received a flyer about an "Infants and Mothers Seminar" to be held at the YWCA. There would be an opportunity to meet other mothers and discuss common issues. Two mothers would be leading the group, and although I was wary of women who would consider themselves authorities on mothering (I had a background in counseling, didn't I?), I decided it wouldn't hurt to give one of them a call.

The woman who answered the phone sounded intelligent without being patronizing. She had a son who was about my daughter's age, and she and another woman had started the group because of a common need for support. The group would meet for an hour and a half for six weeks, and we would bring our children. Each session would be loosely organized around a topic such as physical and emotional changes of postpartum, practical problems, how to deal with infant development, how to balance needs between ourselves and our family, the changing marriage, and the contemporary mother. I decided to sign up, thinking that I could always quit if it didn't work out.

It worked out. The first session was spent in getting acquainted. We had all worked before, but our backgrounds were varied. Our mothering was also different. We measured ourselves against each other at first, reassuring ourselves that at least we didn't have *that* problem. Gradually we came to accept our differences and value the support and sharing.

We didn't have to explain our choice to stay home with our children to each other, yet we were allowed to be ambivalent about our feelings. We were all aware of the frustrations created by the lack of an objective work situation. We knew the defensiveness that could spring up over our husbands' simple question, "What did you do today?" We supported each other through the changes that we were experiencing—financial, and in our relationships with spouses, children, friends, and parents. Through taking turns watching the children in a cooperative play group, we encouraged each other to pursue personal goals in the free time created. As a service to other mothers in our area, we even wrote and published a booklet, *Help, I'm A Mother.*

The group provided the companionship and support I needed at that time. Although I still have many of the feelings mentioned above, and more, I do not feel as alone. I came away with renewed confidence—I'm using the artistic talent that I had allowed to become dormant until I did the illustrations for our booklet, and I am continuing to pursue ways to maintain my personhood within my role as a mother. Although I have moved away from the group, I am more willing to seek the friendship of those I had been trying so hard to be different from—other mothers. □

MOTHERHOOD VS. A CAREER

By Diane Chappell

"What had been, before the baby's birth, an extremely simple plan that I would return to work part-time and hire a sitter, was suddenly complicated by feelings of guilt, resentment, and frustration."

It was my second week home from the hospital. During dinner I turned to my husband, Michael, and said, "I think we should begin looking for a sitter. I'll be returning to work in a little more than four weeks."

We had agreed long before Nicholas was born that I would take a six-week leave of absence after the baby was born and then return part-time to my teaching position. Therefore, I was stunned when he replied, "I don't think you really need to return to your job. We're doing OK financially, and I think the baby needs you here." My mother, who was visiting us and who herself had not returned to her career until the youngest of us was in school, was quick to agree with him. I decided not to press the point until I had my husband alone. Thus began the most emotional and anxiety-ridden period of our marriage.

Throughout our marriage Michael has always been supportive of my being a professional person. He has been understanding and always willing to assume responsibility for at least half of the housework and meal preparation. Needless to say, I was astonished by his new perspective on a woman's place in the family.

Maybe it was the rebel in me reacting against what I felt was unfair pressure from him or maybe it was just postpartum depression, but I was determined to get out of the house and return to my job. I felt that I had left part of my identity there and that I had to retrieve it and come to terms with it. About this time Nicholas grew fussy, and nothing I could do seemed to please him. I began to feel like little more than a vending machine dispensing milk, comfort, and love that was unreciprocated and unappreciated.

I thought of everything I had done to establish my reputation as a teacher, and I wondered what would become of me if I stayed home and cared for my baby and the house for three or four years. Probably in that time we would want another baby, and it might be at least ten years before I could get back to work. The thought of my mind slowly rusting like lawn furniture in winter was depressing. What had been, before the baby's birth, an extremely simple plan that I would return to work part-time and hire a sitter, was suddenly complicated by feelings of guilt, resentment, and frustration.

During my pregnancy I had read everything I could find on childbearing, including Selma Fraiberg's *Every Child's Birthright: In Defense of Mothering*. I agreed with her that in the first years of life it is important for a baby to form a bond with a principal caretaker and that this caretaker is most logically the mother. I didn't think that my working in the mornings would interfere with the establishment of this new bond between me and my baby. I would still be his principal caretaker, and I had decided to breast-feed him for at least the first six months of his life to get him off to the healthiest start possible. His pediatrician had assured me that it would not harm him or undermine our nursing routine if he were to receive one supplemental bottle of formula from his baby-sitter. I did not plan to neglect my baby. Why was I being made to feel guilty by family members and friends who assumed I would?

I finally confronted my husband, and by talking calmly to him, I saw what was troubling him about my returning to work. His primary concern was truly for the baby's welfare, but his reservations about my returning to work had more to do with the threat it posed to our own relationship. He feared that the long hours I would spend grading papers and preparing for class would leave us very little time together. I assured him that this would not be the case, and I made a silent promise to myself to stay organized so my work would not interfere with our time together.

Two weeks before I returned to my job, Michael took a week off from work to get to know our baby. During this time we established a daily routine that we planned to follow when I returned to work. The woman next door, a new mother who had also attended the same prenatal class, agreed to assume the awesome task of caring for two infants. Although we believed that we could find no better sitter for our son, I was torn by anxiety and slept only one hour the night before I returned to work.

That Monday morning was the worst day of my life. We went next door prepared with a long list of emergency numbers, boxes of diapers and baby wipes, cans of formula and sterilized bottles, and enough blankets and changes of clothes for a week. The longest separation I had ever had from my baby before that morning was the hour or two at the grocery store on Saturday mornings. We drove our neighbor crazy those first few days by calling her during our breaks to check on the baby. Fortunately, common sense intervened, and we soon realized that he was in good hands; Nicholas' smiles each morning when we left him with the sitter assured us of that.

Initially, the baby adjusted well to our schedule. He slept most of the morning, and I don't think he was aware the first two months that we were gone. Our afternoons together were wonderful. He was alert, and we played or walked outside when the weather permitted. When he napped, I did either my schoolwork or my housework, or I napped, too, if I was tired. We rarely left him with a baby-sitter on weekends, and we devoted all of our time to being with him. In retrospect I wonder if maybe we didn't spend too much time with him, attempting to overcompensate.

However, four weeks before the end of the school year, we noticed a change in his disposition. He cried in the mornings when we left him, and Monday mornings were particularly grim. He grew restless and whined if I was more than 15 minutes late picking him up. The crying grew worse each morning, and our sense of guilt increased proportionately. Our happy, independent baby was fast becoming a clinging, whining baby. One of us would have to stay home with him. It was only logical that I be the one. I made far less money than Michael, and we could not survive on my salary.

So I resigned from my job, and since then our baby has reverted to his old behavior: he is happy, easy-going, and independent. My being home with him has provided him with the security he needs. He plays by himself a good part of the day, and I am able to write or do my housework while keeping in touch with him. My story is not written to advocate that all new mothers stay home and care for their babies. Like mothers, babies are individuals, and what makes one family happy may not work for another family.

Though I more than occasionally have moments when I feel "trapped" and miss the freedom I enjoyed while being out of the house, we are much happier as a family in this new arrangement. I know that my staying home is not a permanent condition and that when Nick and I are both ready, I will return to work. We have learned that a family relationship doesn't work according to rigid rules and expectations. The needs and desires of each member must be taken into consideration, and the relationship must be flexible for all to be happy. To all new mothers who can choose either to stay at home with a new baby or return to work, I say ignore the books and the advice of well-meaning friends and relatives. Be sensitive to the needs of your baby, and follow your heart. In the long run, only it can tell you what is right. □

NO APPLAUSE

By Cathryn Newman

*"I was afraid that if I went back to see the spring play,
I would wish I was still there directing. But when
the applause quieted down and the students rushed over
for hellos and hugs, I discovered something."*

In the middle of the play I thought of the baby. I wasn't worried, as I had been the first time we left him for the whole day and went skiing. And it wasn't the feeling I had during the first few weeks after he was born, when I went back to work so I could finish the semester. No, it was just a lonely feeling that he was somewhere else, and I wanted to be with him.

I turned my attention back to the play, but I had lost the plot. Only six months ago I had been sitting here nervously mouthing every line as many of these same actors performed in another play. Now I was sitting in the audience, watching students I had taught and directed for three years, producing a play without me. The leading lady, one of my best students, had stood and said, "We'd like to welcome back our old drama teacher." As familiar faces smiled my way and applauded, I somehow wished she had said former and not old.

My decision to give up an eight-year successful teaching career was not an easy one. For years even before I was married, I had thought about motherhood. I always thought I would want to stay home with my children. But for seven years my life revolved around afterschool rehearsals, casting, building sets, and donating many long hours to high-school theater productions. I worked with talented students, helpful parents, an administration that was supportive, and audiences who came year after year to applaud our efforts. I was happy. I loved teaching, and in spite of long hours and discouraging times, I was always eager to begin another year. So when I became pregnant, my decision to quit my job for motherhood came with reluctance.

I took a three-week maternity leave after Jordan was born and then returned to finish the semester. A neighbor took care of him, and I drove home on breaks to breast-feed him. It was a long and difficult eight weeks: I was not prepared for the attention this little person demanded. I thought that if I could handle 60 energetic high school students in a musical, one little baby couldn't be that difficult. The trouble was that I was trying to do both things at once and didn't have the time or the energy. Every night Stan came home to find me in tears. I was uncertain of my decision to quit teaching and fearful of what Jordan was going to do to our security. Mostly, I was tired.

In December Stan accepted a job several hundred miles away, near the small town where I had grown up. We were both excited about the move. It looked like a good position for Stan, and I would enjoy being near my family. I finished my last weeks of school, and we moved in January.

I was so relieved not to be teaching that the first few weeks as a home-maker were a welcome rest. I unpacked slowly and organized our new home carefully. Now that this was to be my career, our home was going to be in better shape. Jordan and I began to develop a relaxed and loving relationship. When Stan came home from work, I usually had a dinner, a nice clean house, and a cared-for baby waiting for him.

Then I ran out of closets. I became bored with housework. I was tired of being home alone all day. I missed the activity and sharing with daily working companions. I couldn't think of anything to do, so I began watching TV and the clock. Days dragged on, and when Stan came home, I was irritable and depressed.

We discussed the possibility of my going back to work. Neither one of us liked how I was feeling. But I remembered those days when I was trying to do both jobs and decided that it was right for me to be home with my son. I wanted to be with him. But I wanted to be happy, and I just didn't know how I was going to do it.

The difficulty of a homemaker's job is that she must be self-motivating. There is no boss to give assignments or deadlines. There are no supervisors. Teaching requires college training and certification. Motherhood requires only that you have a baby, not that you have adequate training for the job. And perhaps the most difficult thing for me to adjust to was no salary. And no applause.

The first problem I dealt with was loneliness. There are millions of women doing the same things each day in different houses, and we need to get together often. Being with others reinforces our efforts and combats loneliness. My church group became a solution for me. Its women's organization meets weekly, and I made many new and interesting friends.

I also became more organized and put myself on a schedule. On Monday evening Stan and I plan our week. We make lists of things we'd like to do. I make a personal list for every day of the week and write things in as I think of them. Some days I only finish one or two things on the list. Other days I throw the whole list away.

There are still many things I dislike about being a homemaker. I often feel defensive about my new status. For example, when we applied for the loan to buy our new home and the loan officer asked if I worked, I almost went into a lengthy explanation of how being a mother was working. At parties I still feel the need to point out that I am college-educated and that I am a homemaker by choice. These are things I hope I can work out within myself.

I am proud of my decision and happy that I am adjusting. I realize that there are advantages and disadvantages to every job, but I miss the excitement of high school students, the challenges and stimulation of my former world. I get homesick for the energy level I had to meet. But I often forget about the discipline problems, the grading periods, and whining, difficult students. It's easy to remember only the good.

The disadvantage of being a homemaker is that no one pays you. The advantage—and main reason for my decision to stay home—is Jordan. I wouldn't trade my experiences with him for anything right now.

I was afraid that if I went back to see the spring play, I would wish I was still there directing. But when the applause quieted down and the students rushed over for hellos and hugs, I discovered something. I did miss them, but not as much as I had missed Jordan earlier that night.

Sometimes in the evening, after a particularly rough day, I long for those audiences who used to applaud my efforts. Today there are only four hands clapping. Two from Stan, and two from a little baby playing pat-a-cake. For today that is enough. □

PATERNITY LEAVE

By Joe Kimball

"I had taken an unpaid paternity leave from my job as a newspaper reporter for three reasons: to help my wife adjust to two tiny children; to help the children adjust to each other; and to give myself the opportunity to see my girls growing up."

The baby was screaming as her eighteen-month-old sister toddled around the kitchen, slowly emptying a cup of milk on the floor. All their toys were strewn on the bedroom floor, and seven diapers lay stacked in the bathroom, waiting to be rinsed out, if I could just find the time.

But there wasn't time, just then. With the baby under one arm and the toddler underfoot, I was struggling with dinner—juggling pans of potatoes, gravy, and corn, with chicken in the oven—hoping at least three of the four would be ready at the same time.

My wife was supposed to be home at 6:30. At 6:25 the potatoes looked done, the chicken was crispy, and the corn started to boil. But when she got home 30 minutes later, the chicken was burned and so was I. And more diapers had been added to the pile in the bathroom, waiting to be rinsed out.

Looking back now, that incident is an accurate reminder of what I was doing. I had taken an unpaid paternity leave from my job as a newspaper reporter for three reasons: to help my wife adjust to two tiny children; to help the children adjust to each other; and to give myself the opportunity to see my girls growing up.

Not everyone understood why I wanted to take a paternity leave when my second daughter was born in February. "You must be crazy," said a male co-worker. "When my kids were born, I kissed my wife good-by and took off on a two-week business trip."

That's the way it used to be and still is in many families. Raising the children was Mother's job, something only a woman could do well. Father might change a diaper or heat up the formula in the middle of the night, but in the morning he was off to work—and guess who was left holding the soiled diapers and dirty bottles?

But that concept is changing these days. For one thing, women make up more than 40 percent of the work force in the United States, so part of the responsibility and satisfaction of child rearing is shifting from mother to child-care centers and baby-sitters. That has made some fathers ask why they can't take a more active role in raising our children. Fathers are parents too.

Equality is one of the issues touted by some advocates of shared child rearing. Mothers, like fathers, should be free to have a career outside the home. And fathers should be free to stay home with the children. This idea— househusbands at home taking care of the house and the kids—hasn't caught on big yet, but it may end up being the ultimate argument in the equal rights battle.

My plan was less dramatic than that. I, too, wanted to get involved in raising the children—but without drastically upsetting the balance of our traditional family.

When our oldest daughter was born, my wife, Barbara, gave up a full-time job to stay home with her. Except for the usual inconveniences and middle-of-the-night feedings, Barbara liked being a full-time mother and decided to put off any career plans until the children were in school.

I had been in the delivery room during the birth, coaching Barbara during labor and cutting the umbilical cord. I got up at night with the baby, except when I had to be at work early in the morning, and did all the other traditional paternal duties. I thought I was doing my share. I wanted to do more, though, when we learned that our second child was on its way.

Barbara told me about the new baby after I returned from an out-of-town assignment. Not only had I been gone when she first learned she was pregnant, but also my daughter had taken her first steps while I was away. I was disappointed and felt left out. I'd missed two of the big moments in a young father's life.

My daughter would be seventeen months old when the new baby was due. "Two in diapers—good luck," friends said. "You're going to have your hands full," my mother warned. But the way it looked, they wouldn't be my hands. I'd be going to work each morning leaving two, maybe three, crying persons behind. It didn't seem fair. Until then, I had never heard of a paternity leave.

Everyone knows about maternity leaves—mothers take some time off after their baby is born and either decide to quit their jobs or go back to work. Fathers? Sometimes they take a week off to take care of the other children while the mother and new baby are in the hospital. But that's usually all.

I decided to ask for a three-month paternity leave. My company offers a six-month, unpaid maternity leave to women having babies. Generally women are considered medically disabled for about two months after childbirth. I figured the company was offering women two months' leave related to childbirth and four months' child-raising leave. So I, too, should be eligible for some time off, I thought.

The company didn't see things that way. When I formally applied for a three-month paternity leave, I was turned down. Instead they said they would consider offering me a one-month personal leave if my job performance was satisfactory in the three months before the baby was due.

I didn't think that was fair, so I filed a sex discrimination complaint with the Minnesota Department of Human Rights. It was the first "paternity leave" complaint ever filed in the state, officials said.

The company lawyers and I outlined our positions for the hearing held in my case. The commissioner of human rights must now determine whether I was discriminated against. If so, the state will bring suit, on my behalf, against the company. Even if such a suit results and I should win, I stand to win nothing tangible (unless we have another baby while I'm still working for the company). But the case could prove important to other fathers who want time at home with their children.

The legal issues, although important for me and as a possible precedent in future cases, became secondary when my daughter was born. The next day I was offered the one-month personal leave. I took it. I also scheduled three weeks of vacation to begin when the leave ended, so for seven weeks I was a full-time, at-home daddy.

The first few days were hectic, and like most new fathers, I spent much of my time shuttling between the hospital and fast-food restaurants.

It wasn't until Barbara and the baby came home, though, that the importance of my leave became apparent. Though we thought we had fully prepared Joey, our toddler, for the new baby, she sometimes seemed personally offended when the baby wouldn't stop crying. Sometimes she would lash out at the baby with her hand, not maliciously, but in frustration.

We hoped that a little extra love and reassurance would solve the problem, so Barbara and I made sure that we set aside certain times of the day to spend individually with the girls. We also set a time each day for Barbara to get out of the house alone, away from the tension that inevitably builds in a situation with a hungry baby, a mischievous toddler, and a fussy husband.

I had to get away from it all at times too. Being home was quite unlike a job, where you can go out to lunch to get away from the pressures. My pressures were now with me at lunch and each day, and no problem at work ever seemed as hopeless as the nights the baby refused to go back to sleep after her 3 a.m. feeding. To escape, I would send the three of them shopping so I could have a couple of hours of quiet to read; and once a week I would meet friends or co-workers for lunch.

The best part of my time at home, though, was the time we spent together. Even (I never thought I'd be saying this) those late nights and early mornings. For the first few weeks, when the baby cried for her feedings at night, she woke Joey, who would join in. So we'd all be up, rocking and singing together.

Barbara and I divided up the chores at home. It took two loads of laundry before I knew the difference between detergent and bleach, and it wasn't until Barbara overheard me and a bachelor friend comparing the merits of the new liquid detergents that she knew the clothes (and the washing machine) were safe.

The other jobs we divided up as they came. Whoever had a girl with a dirty diaper would change her. Cleaning and vacuuming were done by the one with a free moment. And free moments were at a premium at our house.

When I was alone with the girls and both were crying, I would count the days until my leave was over and I could return to the adult world. But those feelings came rarely and always disappeared when one of the girls fell asleep in my arms.

Occasionally during my leave, I would prepare a meal, but normally that was done by Barb, who is a much better cook. Because I'm a better baker, I made all the cookies, cakes, and bread. In fact, one morning my mother called to ask for a recipe for cookies I had made. I was happy to oblige.

But that night, while Barb and I were folding some clothes, she turned to me and said, "The clothes always smell so fresh when you wash them." "That does it," I joked. "It's time to go back to work. No one should be made to feel like a television commercial twice in one week."

By then there were only three days left until I returned to work. Two strong emotions tugged at me—the satisfaction of spending time with the girls and helping Barb versus the challenges and social interaction of work.

Of course, work won, helped immeasurably by the lure of the paycheck. But that time at home brought me closer than ever to my family, and I'd do it again in a minute. ☐

THE JOB AND BABY DILEMMA

By Anita Lienert

"At first the answer seemed obvious: return to work. Daniel cried half the night and ate around the clock. Any job would be a cinch compared to the demands of a newborn."

I didn't have to wait until my son was born to experience the agony of deciding whether or not to work outside the home. That conflict started the first day I found out I was pregnant.

The doctor called in the morning to tell me my pregnancy test was positive. I was still reeling from the news that afternoon when I got another phone call—the offer of a long-awaited job transfer to Washington, D.C.

Both shocking bits of news kept Paul and me up for most of that hot summer night. Having a baby seemed all wrong at this time. We had only been married for two months and had not planned on starting a family so soon. Paul had just been promoted and often spent weeks away from home on business trips. My own career as a reporter was clicking along. And as newlyweds, we were only beginning to adjust to each other. For hours we agonized over whether I should accept the transfer or even continue to work. It was clear that the simple act of giving birth was going to have staggering repercussions.

But we had looked forward to starting a family in a few years, and our timetable was the only thing that had changed. By the time we drifted off to sleep that night, we agreed that we were delighted at the prospect of a new baby, and we promised each other that neither of our careers would suffer just because we were about to become parents. "Compromise is all it takes," Paul assured me.

The next morning I turned down the offer—with more than a twinge of regret—to transfer out of the Detroit office of the magazine where I had been a reporter for two years, and cover Congress in Washington. Accepting it would be a mistake, I thought, because I doubted whether I could keep my active pace as the pregnancy advanced. And I didn't want to do anything to jeopardize my baby's health.

As the summer passed, I was overjoyed at how little my pregnancy affected my job. Sometimes I'd get slightly nauseated when I had to fly to assignments out of town, but otherwise things went smoothly. Both Paul and my doctor encouraged me to continue working as long as I could before the baby was born.

But what about afterwards? The subject came up again and again, especially when we began taking childbirth classes at the local hospital. Most of the other nine couples in the class were also mulling over the issue of whether or not the new mother should work. Next to concerns about delivery, it was the most talked-about subject in the class. The nurse in charge of the class shared her experiences with us. When her two children were infants, she had worked the midnight shift while her husband had worked in the daytime, and they had split the child-care duties. "It brought us closer together," she reported. But few of the couples in the class—including us—were able to juggle their work hours like that. Paul and I decided to postpone the crucial decision until the baby arrived.

Several weeks before my due date, I began my maternity leave. I wondered if I would feel claustrophobic spending most of my time at home and whether I would itch to get back to the outside world. As it happened, I was grateful for time to relax and work on pet projects, such as refinishing an old bookcase and painting the laundry room. The time flew by until March when Daniel was born. From that day I had six weeks of maternity leave left to decide whether or not to return to work.

At first the answer seemed obvious: return to work. Daniel cried half the night and ate around the clock. Any job would be a cinch compared to the demands of a newborn. And it didn't seem to matter to Daniel who fed or changed him. He reacted just about the same to everyone. I thought that any sitter who was efficient and kind could do the job as well as I did. Besides, I had spent four years in college training for my profession and five years on the job. I resented my son's interfering with my career. During the first two weeks of Daniel's life, I was certain that I would be back at my desk in a short time. Then things began to change.

Daniel began to eat a little cereal during the day and started to sleep most of the night. Since I wasn't as exhausted as I had been during the first few weeks, I enjoyed him more. He started to notice things and take on a personality. He was fascinated by bright lights. He seemed to enjoy his bath. And he gave me a big smile when he was only a month old. And he didn't smile at just anybody either. He was getting to know me and was showing me that he liked me. I put in a request for a three-month extension on my maternity leave and got it. I needed more time to decide.

I sought out other new mothers to find out how they were handling the dilemma of motherhood and career. I got a lot of insights but few pat answers. One of the mothers I talked to was a medical technologist with a nine-month-old daughter. She went back to her ten-hour-a-day job when her child was two months old. "I don't regret it at all," she said. "I think my daughter is learning to accept strangers and is not clinging to me. I'm more relaxed when I'm with her, and the lady next door takes excellent care of her."

Another mother in our neighborhood, who has a three-month-old son, decided not to return to her secretarial job. "We're learning to live on one paycheck, and I think it's important for me to be home during the first years to let my son know there's someone around he can trust." A third mother I talked to tried working but gave it up to devote full-time to her infant. Her concern centered around how sitters were treating her child. "A child can't tell what kind of treatment he's getting when he can barely say 'Mama,'" she said.

After talking to several mothers, I found that the choice to work or not is never simple. Despite what I learned from them, I had to follow my own instincts. I was still torn between devoting most of my time to Daniel or trying to juggle both a job and motherhood.

I experimented with baby-sitters. Relatives offered to watch the baby while I returned to work, but the experiences I had with them up to that point were often fraught with friction. They interfered with my methods and complained about everything from the temperature in the nursery to the type of formula I used. It wasn't worth constant haggling with them in order to return to work. Outside sitters took good care of Daniel, but they were sometimes undependable. And Daniel was too young to be enrolled in a day care center.

Paul and I spent countless hours talking about the turmoil I was going through. He even offered to quit his job and stay home with Daniel while I returned to work. After all, there was virtually no difference in our incomes. Still, that plan just didn't feel right to me. The truth is, I was finding that taking care of Daniel was as interesting and challenging as any job I'd ever held.

By the time he was three months old, Daniel liked to vocalize and socialize. He could tell a familiar face from a strange one and occasionally cried at strange faces and surroundings. He stared intently at trees and leaves blowing in the breeze when he went for a buggy ride. He started to cut his first tooth.

Returning to work made less sense than ever. Even economically, it seemed to be a mistake to return to work. A sitter's salary, clothing, food, and commuting expenses plus taxes would eat up almost half of my income. I would be left with more job satisfaction than money in the bank. But more importantly, Daniel seemed to need me. He prospered during his first three months, and I wanted to ensure his continued growth.

A final bit of advice came from my pediatrician. He encouraged me to maintain outside interests to keep my mind stimulated and to make sure the bonds don't get too tight between my son and me. But as for a full-time job, he said, "Unless you have an urgent money need, the child should take precedence."

After a lot of soul-searching, I have decided not to return to work full-time. It's a decision I will probably consider again. I may decide to work part-time when Daniel is six or seven months old. I may go back to college at night.

As for now, I try to get out of the house once or twice a week so Daniel and I don't get too dependent on each other. This is the decision I'm most comfortable with. Some of my co-workers have asked whether I'm "dropping out" or "copping out." I simply tell them that raising my son is my "new job." □

CHAPTER 4
PARENTING PROBLEMS AND SOLUTIONS

A PERFECT MOTHER

By Barbara Wolfe

*"I waded through pages of feeding problems and discipline problems,
heredity versus environment, demand versus schedule—
all the while sinking deeper into the mud of confusion until
I was sure I couldn't learn it all in time."*

What happens when a mother-to-be doesn't know the first thing about babies? I guess she has to learn in a hurry, right? Well, that's exactly what I tried to do. I bought the best-selling books and listened to everyone's advice. But in a few months, I realized that my own baby taught me more than the stack of books or the whole crowd of relatives.

In my case I had even more to learn than most people. I grew up with two older sisters but never got the little brother or sister I used to ask Mom for. There weren't many kids in the neighborhood, and my relatives lived far away. So I never managed to be around babies much. As a result, I learned to feel very shy and awkward with babies and toddlers. I didn't know what to say to them or how to amuse them; I was too self-conscious to make funny faces and ridiculous noises. Whenever I held a baby, he would sense my nervousness and begin to bawl immediately. This was a catastrophe! I told myself I wasn't equipped to handle babies.

On the rare occasions that someone did bring a baby around, I'd admire him from a distance and make every excuse not to handle him. When I was little, saying I was afraid I'd drop him was enough. But when I reached my teens, people assumed that any girl my age was dying to hold and cuddle their baby. So I invented more creative excuses, like, "Oh, I'd love to, but I just got over a cold, and I don't dare!" Most people settled for that excuse, and I used it quite often.

Finally, I met up with a baby that I couldn't run away from—my own. Our child was coming along about five years sooner than we had planned. We were happy and excited, but I felt pretty worried too. Suddenly I needed to know everything about babies; I had to make up for all those years of running away from kids.

My first impulse was to snatch up every child-care book I could find. In a few weeks I had my own library. I waded through pages of feeding problems and discipline problems, heredity versus environment, demand versus schedule—all the while sinking deeper into the mud of confusion until I was sure I couldn't learn it all in time. My husband pleaded with me to put the books away and relax, but I was already addicted.

Next, I developed a craving to have everything ready for the baby, long before he was due. After reading that all baby items should be washed before use, I hauled my seven dozen (that's 84) diapers to the laundromat. There, I washed and rinsed them, and washed and rinsed them again, much to the dismay of the people waiting for an empty machine. I folded each diaper with mathematical precision and arranged them all into snowy white stacks. When every stitch of clothing was likewise washed and folded, I relaxed by making crib mobiles and hanging up cheerful posters. And after I could do no more, I still found things to do.

After all the usual lumps, bumps, aches, and pains, Timmy was born, exactly on his due date. He promised to be a very cooperative baby. Together we would do everything by the book, obey all rules, and be the most adorable mother and child in recorded history. People would describe me as a loving and gentle mother, a creative homemaker, an exciting hostess, but most of all, just a fantastic person in general.

Oh, I'd like to say every dream came true, but that's not the way it was. At first Timmy was no more trouble than a baby doll. He ate well and slept a lot. We marveled over our little beauty as he slept, and we snapped pictures when he awoke. We mailed out birth announcements and reaped a crop of baby gifts. We rocked him and cuddled him, and things were just heavenly. For a few days, that is.

I had read about postpartum depression but figured that since I knew about it, I'd be able to sail right through it without a tear. I heard that a new father can feel jealous and left out but decided I'd simply get my husband involved and there would be no problem.

I remember days when I barely had time to wash my face. Timmy hustled me through the day like a drill instructor in the Marines. "Feed me, hold me, change me, wash my diapers, rock me to sleep, feed me—right now!" His crying drove me up the wall. Some days we cried together. I recognized my depression as the baby blues, but pinning a name to it didn't cheer me up much.

As for my husband, he did feel left out and jealous. Who could blame him? Timmy had a knack of interrupting us at the worst possible moments, and I had a habit of running straight to him. Every time I fixed a good supper, the baby cried, my husband ate alone, and it was cold by the time I reached it. Quiet conversations were a thing of the past. So were the mornings we used to snuggle in bed and be lazy till noon. Since I was breast-feeding and Timmy didn't seem to like formula, I hated to leave him with a sitter. Gone were the days when we could jump in the car to get ice cream or just ride around. My husband still needed his wife, but the baby needed his mother. How could I be in two places at once? Even though he loved his baby son, he resented him for stealing me away. I discovered that getting a husband involved with the baby isn't as simple as letting him change a few diapers.

Things were clearly not going the way I had planned. To add to my confusion, visitors began to drop in with the last thing any new mother needs—advice. "Advice" is my polite way of saying "criticism." Aunt Ethel assured me that I didn't have enough clothes on the baby; Uncle Leroy said he looked hot. Betty Lou said he must surely be eating mashed potatoes by now. "When do you plan to stop breast-feeding and give the child some real food?" "Why is he coughing?" "Hasn't he started to roll over yet?" All these comments left me feeling confused and angry. But even though I resented advice, I took every word to heart and couldn't ignore it.

To my satisfaction and the dismay of the doomsday crowd, each visit to the pediatrician revealed that Timmy was perfectly healthy, normal, and content, and that I was obviously doing a good job as a mother. I rejoiced.

Eventually, the books began to gather dust on the shelf. I found that I could let a whole week slide by without consulting the experts. The stream of unasked-for advice began to flow in one ear and out the other. The pieces started to fit together again. Time, patience, and a little baby named Timmy were teaching me all I needed to know. I learned by trial and error. Sure, I made plenty of mistakes, but Timmy didn't hold them against me. For all Timmy knew, I was the best mommy in the world, and after a while, I began to think maybe he was right.

My husband and I learned to accept the changes in our life. In order to get things done, we had to plan our time more carefully. That meant no more breakfasts at noon and no more dashes to the beach at a moment's notice. After trying to take Timmy along wherever we went, I realized we needed a babysitter. It nearly broke my heart the first few times we left him behind, but it got easier with practice. We cherished our time alone, and the time off recharged me for another round of diapers and demands. The less I fussed and worried about our baby, the more we enjoyed him.

My baby really isn't a baby anymore—he's an energetic toddler. We've both done a lot of growing this year. I've learned that a sense of motherhood can't be had for the price of a book. The job requires common sense, patience, and the strong desire to be a good mother. Without these things, the books, the advice, the pretty mobiles, and the snowy white diapers are practically useless. So why try to be the "perfect" mother? My baby taught me that just being a good mother is better! Relax, enjoy, and let your baby teach you. □

BAD WORDS VS. GOOD WORDS

By Dianne Koehnecke

"But now, here we were, in a new place, faced with the major adjustments of moving, and we had the dilemma of our son's language to cope with besides. Our minds were on getting settled, not on settling him."

When we moved to a different part of the country and a new neighbor came over with coffee and cookies, my two-year-old son greeted her but not in the usual way. Instead of "hello" or even "hi," he spurted out some words that I never knew he knew. They were not nice words. You could call them obscene.

How did my sweet, lovable two-year-old pick up such a vocabulary? If my neighbor was shocked, she wasn't the only one. I felt my face turn from pink to red to purple. The neighbor told me she had an eighteen-month-old son, and I wondered if she would ever allow her boy to play with mine. I wouldn't blame her if she didn't.

Where in the world did my son learn those words? I thought back to the time when, in a fit of desperation after listening to our dog bark incessantly for five minutes, I had yelled out, "Shut up!" I remembered the little boys in our old neighborhood shouting out some words I had heard my son say to our new neighbors that morning. I thought about the mover who had uttered profanities when the dresser he was carrying scratched a wall.

My son had heard those words, but he hadn't used any of them. Now, suddenly, he seemed to remember them all, and he began to use them in the right places at all the wrong times, such as the time in the grocery store when I told him he couldn't have any cookies; or in the restaurant when his dad told him not to spill his food.

He tried out his newly acquired vocabulary on anyone and everyone. Keeping him home wasn't safe either. The appliance man, the realtor, the interior decorator, the garbage collectors—all who entered our house were fair game. As soon as he met any new person, he seemed to feel a need to show off his wanton words.

He had a definite problem, and his problem was affecting the entire family. What were we going to do with him? It seemed as if he had become a different person overnight. He loved to shock everyone with his new words. Even if the attention he got was negative, it seemed to satisfy him.

If he hadn't been such a little angel up to this time, maybe it wouldn't have bothered me so much. But he had been such a sweet little guy. Oh, he'd had his moments, like the day he dumped the gasoline over the garage floor, or the time he got into my lipstick and decorated the bathroom floor with it, but by and large, he was good. At least his language had always been good.

But now, here we were, in a new place, faced with the major adjustments of moving, and we had the dilemma of our son's language to cope with besides. Our minds were on getting settled, not on settling him.

Still, we knew something *had* to be done. We didn't want him to be ostracized by all the neighborhood kids. We didn't want him to get glaring looks from the people in grocery stores and restaurants.

What we did want was a little boy who didn't swear, who didn't say "shut up," and who didn't shock strangers with his lamentable language.

We began trying out a variety of disciplinary methods. The first kind of punishment we used was the good old-fashioned spanking. We spanked, and we spanked, *and* we spanked. But instead of curing the curses, the spanking just seemed to increase them. His vocabulary worsened with each stroke.

Next we tried the punishment of deprivation. "If you don't stop saying those bad words, you can't have your banana," we would threaten. Unfortunately, our son didn't mind not getting his banana, or playing with his new toy, or having to stay indoors all afternoon. He preferred to continue to use the words we had come to detest.

He was getting on everyone's nerves, and we wondered if there would ever be an end to it. One day the same new neighbor who had greeted us with coffee and cookies was brave enough to return with her eighteen-month-old son. Sure enough, my son's vocabulary was the worst it had ever been. I was even more embarrassed than I had been the first time the neighbor had heard his deplorable dialogue, because this time every kind of punishment I used failed to work. Not only was my child using bad language, but also he was ignoring my methods to get him to stop.

"Why don't you try ignoring him?" my neighbor suggested. For two days I did just that. But after 48 long hours of suffering, my ears couldn't take it anymore. Ignoring his bad words didn't make them go away.

I tried another tactic. "Would you please stop saying those bad words?" I began asking my son. I continued with kind words, politely requesting him to stop swearing.

He refused even my reasonable, kind requests. By this time I was getting desperate. Then my parents came for a holiday visit.

My son promptly began showing off his newly acquired vocabulary for them. I promptly explained the situation and told them how frustrated the language had made all of us.

"Have you tried behavior modification?" my mom, the elementary school teacher, asked me.

"What's that?" I wanted to know. It had been a few years since I had been in the classroom, and behavior modification was a new term to me, but I was willing to try anything.

"What it means," Mom explained, "is to encourage the child to change *on his own*. Instead of negative punishment, you try to get the child to stop whatever bad or irritable thing he is doing by encouraging the good things he does."

"How can I do that?" I asked her.

"Mainly, you praise the good. When he says good words, or even normal words, you praise him. You give him the attention he is seeking but not when he's doing something you *don't* want him to do. You give him encouragement and praise when he's doing what you *do* want him to do."

"That sounds a little complicated," I said. "Could you give me an example?"

At that moment my son walked into the room. "Gwama, weed me a stawee," he asked my mother.

"Certainly I will because you are saying such *nice* words. You asked Grandma to read you a story so nicely. You are such a good boy to say such nice words."

My mother looked at me, and I nodded. Her approach was beginning to sink in. She proceeded to read my son a story while I thought about her idea. Would the behavior modification technique work?

For the next few days, I began to pay attention to my son when he was behaving, instead of giving him attention during the negative confrontations.

"Mommy, kin I have a cooky?" my son would ask.

"You sure can because you said such nice words," I would respond.

When the bad words came, as they inevitably did, I did not shout or scold, or even ignore. I explained to my son, "Mommy does not like to hear bad words. They hurt Mommy's ears. Mommy likes to hear nice words. Can you say some nice words?"

"Nice wads?" my son would ask.

"Yes, nice words like 'I love you' or 'thank you.'"

"I love you. Sank you," he repeated.

I promptly gave my son a big kiss and a hug too. "Such nice words," I praised him.

Day by day the bad words dwindled, and the good words multiplied. By the end of the month, my son was sounding normal again, and the rest of the family was beginning to feel normal.

Behavior modification using positive reinforcement sounds very technical. But seeking a change in a child's behavior by using praise and encouragement doesn't seem difficult.

It wasn't for me. And more important, it solved my problem. □

BALANCING FANTASY AND REALITY

By Lucille Doggett

"And we learned that the special quality which allows young children to imagine that forest animals talk and that the clouds are crying when it rains, will not last forever."

Before my children were even born, I'd decided that I was going to raise them with strict doses of reality. As far as I was concerned, letting children indulge too much in their imaginations resulted in a distorted view of the world. I was determined to be totally honest with my children and to expect total honesty from them.

But then one day my two-year-old daughter, Dana, made a discovery. She was busy emptying my dresser drawers—a favorite occupation of hers—when she found an old, fuzzy, black ski hat that I had worn years ago.

"Look, look what I found, Mommy," Dana cried, waving the hat in the air.

"Oh, that's my old ski hat," I remarked.

"No, it's not!" she exclaimed stubbornly. "It's a kitty cat. It's my black, fuzzy kitty cat."

Then carefully rolling the hat into a ball and stroking it gently, Dana disappeared into her bedroom with her new treasure. Later, when I came to claim my old hat and return it to the drawer, my daughter clutched it tightly and cried, "No, no, Mommy, this is kitty. She doesn't want to stay in the drawer anymore. She wants to sleep on my bed."

My child's pleasure in her new toy was so touching that I decided to let her play with it a bit longer. "What's the kitty's name?" I asked.

"Her name's Puffo," my little girl replied softly. "And she is a very special kitty. She's all mine, and she's two years old just like me."

That night as she snuggled in her bed, Dana was still clutching the fuzzy ball, smoothing out the long strings that used to keep the hat tied to my head.

"Puffo has two tails, Mommy," Dana remarked, "and she wants to sleep with me."

"Well, I suppose she can sleep in your bed tonight," I replied, falling in with my child's game. "But tomorrow I think she should hop back into the drawer."

"Puffo doesn't like the drawer anymore, Mommy. She wants to sleep with me," murmured Dana, snuggling herself under the covers and cradling the old hat.

Of course, "Puffo" never found her way back into my drawer. The hat became a cat in my daughter's eyes and never lost that identity. Puffo also became an indispensable toy. Besides accompanying my daughter to bed every night, Puffo also kept Dana company during the day. The "kitty" was wheeled about in the old baby stroller, taken on long auto rides to Grandma's house, talked to, stroked, and loved.

We all know (from Dr. Spock and the Linus character of the *Peanuts* comic strip) that small children often develop an intense attachment to one particular object. Some children want to carry the object everywhere and refuse to go to bed without it. Others become so attached to their object that they won't allow it to be cleaned, even though it's been dragged around the backyard every afternoon for a week. The object acquires a life of its own, and the child sees this precious possession as something special and private to be hugged and talked to, especially at bedtime.

Obviously, my child's precious object was Puffo. I recognized her need for such a comforter and felt that I would be depriving her of something special if I took it away and insisted that Puffo was nothing but an old ski hat. But at the same time I wondered if I should encourage her in this fantasy. What about all of my resolutions about raising children to face reality by always insisting on the truth? Suppose that Dana should become dependent on Puffo for years? How could I ever get that hat away from Dana without upsetting her terribly?

Dana's attachment to her kitty was so great that I decided not to relegate Puffo back to the drawer immediately. I would let my child enjoy the pleasure and security she derived from having her "cat." But I would also remind her from time to time of Puffo's real identity, for perhaps as Dana grew older, she might not need Puffo all the time. So I decided to wait a bit and try a gentle approach.

One day Puffo was curled up on the bed while Dana was coloring. By this time Dana had had her third birthday (and coincidentally, Puffo had also become three years old, I had been told). I picked up Puffo and said to my daughter, "Dana, did you know that once upon a time Puffo went skiing with Mommy?"

"Why?" demanded my child in the manner typical of all three-year-olds.

"Because Puffo is really a ski hat, honey," I said, and then I tried it on.

The sight of Puffo sitting on Mommy's head brought shrieks of laughter from my daughter. Then Dana had to try on Puffo herself and look at the results in a mirror. More laughter.

"So you see, honey," I remarked, "Puffo is really a hat."

Dana looked me straight in the eye. "I know that, Mommy, but we can still pretend Puffo is a kitty."

Dana removed the hat from her head and rolled it into a ball and stroked it. "I love Puffo, Mommy," she said, and gently laid her "kitty" on the bed. Even though Dana knew that Puffo was not a real cat, she still wasn't ready to give up the idea entirely. I felt satisfied that Dana understood that her idea of Puffo *was* a fantasy, but that she was still enjoying her game.

And it turned into a game that was shared and enjoyed by the whole family. We all started referring to that old hat as "Puffo." However, to keep a balance between the fantasy and reality of the situation, we would periodically discuss the fact that Puffo wasn't a real cat, but that we liked to pretend about it. And we learned that the special quality which allows young children to imagine that forest animals talk and that the clouds are crying when it rains, will not last forever.

Gradually, Puffo lost some of her magic allure. Dana started going to nursery school. I explained that Puffo was happier sleeping on Dana's bed and waiting for her to return, rather than going along. Dana agreed.

Puffo spends a lot of time curled upon Dana's bed these days. New friends and experiences are opening a wider world for my daughter. But when bedtime comes, the little hands curl the old hat into a ball and start stroking it gently as I turn out the light.

"Tell me a Puffo story, Mommy," Dana says.

And so I find myself aiding and abetting Dana's imagination! I seem to be doing the very thing I always swore I wouldn't do. But I feel that my change in attitude is definitely for the best. Would it help Dana if I never allowed her the pleasure and enjoyment of Puffo? No it wouldn't. In fact, I'd be taking a very special part of childhood away from her. Having Puffo will not distort Dana's sense of reality. It may enhance it, for as she grows older, Puffo helps her see the difference between fantasy and reality.

As Dana's birthday is approaching, I asked her one day, "Dana, will Puffo be four years old on your birthday too?"

"Oh, Mommy," she said impatiently, "Puffo can't have a birthday. Puffo is not a real kitty."

And so I know that my daughter is growing up. How glad I am that Dana found Puffo and loved her, not only for my child's sake, but for my own, for I now realize that young children need these fantasies that allow them to indulge their imaginations. Such fantasies don't mean that they will be untruthful later in life.

A precious part of Dana's childhood is being left behind now. Ahead of us are all those hectic school years of girl scouts and music lessons. I expect to find something to enjoy in every phase of my child's development, but I know that I'll look back on the years that Puffo lived with us as being special years indeed.   □

CALMING THE TEARS OF CHILDHOOD

By Barbara J. Wenger

"How I hit upon my solution of creative storytelling, I can't remember. All I know is that it probably saved my sanity, along with providing some entertaining times for the rest of the family."

What does a mother do when she has held a screaming two-year-old on her lap for what seemed like hours (and may have only been 15 minutes)? When all her strategies and ploys have failed; when she has sung, rocked, bribed, done everything she can possibly think of, and still the child cries and cries and cries. Well, she can lock herself in the bathroom and run water to drown out the noise of his bellowing. Or she can go about her housework trying (probably unsuccessfully) to block out the piercing sounds. If she is lucky, she might be able to hit on a solution that will magically dry up his tears. That's what happened to me when I discovered a new approach that finally worked to quiet my son.

After two sweet-tempered daughters, whose sobs generally subsided at the first strains of "Hush Little Baby," I was more than a little disturbed to have a child whose howlings seemed to have no "off" button. Now I know that it is psychologically sound to let a child cry on occasion; that crying is a very important part of his or her development; that learning to cope with disappointment, anger, fear, and pain is important and is appropriately expressed through tears. But there is a limit to what parents can take. It was hard for me to desert my two-year-old son as he brokenheartedly sobbed over a skinned knee or elbow, or to let him cry himself out after half an hour of rebuffed attempts at comfort. How I hit upon my solution of creative storytelling, I can't remember. All I know is that it probably saved my sanity, along with providing some entertaining times for the rest of the family.

At about six months of age, our son, Jake, began to get hair that, instead of lying flat on his head as his two sisters felt it should, grew straight up and kept on growing. They decided he must be growing a crop of fuzz, so they named him the "Fuzz Farm Boy."

And so it was that the Fuzz Farm Boy began to have adventures— adventures created out of pure desperation as I held and rocked that tiny, damp two-year-old. And he actually responded. His sobs would subside so that he could hear the story, and by the end of it, he had forgotten his anguish. This seemed to me to be nothing short of a miracle, and yet I think it was a simple matter of being able to get his attention. And whose attention would not be held by a story in which he was the main character; in which he could do anything; in which he was a super-hero—even though he had not yet been exposed to the adventures of Batman or the Incredible Hulk.

The stories were surprisingly easy to create. As he grew older, he began to help shape their course. They all started out the same way: "One morning the Fuzz Farm Boy woke up. He jumped out of bed and ran to his window. And what do you think he saw?"

Depending, of course, on how ready Jake was to be consoled, it was at this point that he would begin to fill in the adventure. The Fuzz Farm Boy has seen snow up to the eaves on a June day; he has seen elephants, bears, a hippopotamus, a giraffe, and less exotic creatures—sometimes in zany predicaments, sometimes in greatest peril, and sometimes performing rather mundane actions, like taking down Mother's wash and trampling it in the mud. The Fuzz Farm Boy has rescued kittens from the stomach of a repentant rhinoceros; has dug from his sandbox to China and been back in time for lunch; has gotten lost and ridden home on a fire engine. He has dealt with Dracula, has met Superman and the Hardy Boys, and has helped a lonely and frightened gorilla find his way back to the city zoo.

Most of the stories start out with no end in mind. They ramble on as need be until finally it is time to fix dinner, time to help with someone else's homework, or just time for mother's time. And then they end, appropriately and happily, with a smile on the real Fuzz Farm Boy's face.

Most of the stories have no moral, no hidden meaning. They are just silly and fun—the sillier the better—as any mother of young children soon comes to realize. But there came a time in Jake's life when the tales helped to make him feel more comfortable in strange surroundings or when he was undergoing a frightening experience.

One such experience occurred not long ago, when my husband and I sat with Jake in the waiting room of the local hospital x-ray department. He had just fractured a bone playing football with a friend, and in addition to the pain he was feeling, we noticed that he was extremely uneasy about what lay behind those closed doors. It would have been simple to explain the x-ray procedure to him, and I'm sure he would have felt more at ease. But it was much more fun to tell him about how the Fuzz Farm Boy had once coped with the same situation after being tackled and sat upon by a brown bear who appeared in his backyard one day—a bear who turned out to be a member of the Chicago Bears football team. When it was Jake's turn to go behind those closed doors, he knew just what to expect. The situation had been changed from one that was frightening and unknown to one that was understandable and full of some humor and sympathy for the Fuzz Farm Boy. (After all, Jake had only been sat upon by his best friend and not an 837-pound bear!)

Now the Fuzz Farm Tales have become an important part of family times. They take on a hilarious new aspect with all five of us contributing to their outcome. They, along with other freshly invented stories, help to wile away the time on the long trip between home and Grandmother's house.

Jake is now five and seldom needs a Fuzz Farm Tale to take his mind off his tears. He has become a reasonable child, who cries for a reasonable length of time and then goes back to the more important things in life. But there are times when we still enjoy the fun of telling these tales together: when we are bored; when we want to have some peace and quiet together; when we want to laugh, to feel close, and to explore the wonderful world of the impossible.

Everyone needs to find his or her own way of coping with the tears of childhood. The Fuzz Farm Boy Tales did not always work. Sometimes nothing did. Sometimes a child needs to be left alone with his tears. In cases like that, there is always the bathroom and lots of running water. □

CONQUERING OVERPROTECTIVENESS

By Annette Nolan

"I began to feel that motherhood was an overwhelming burden. It seemed that other mothers enjoyed their babies, while I spent most of my time worrying."

When I became pregnant, I thought I was prepared to be a mother. My husband and I discussed parenthood many times, and we thought we could handle it competently and confidently. I planned to quit my job and stay home with the baby, and my husband would help in the evenings and take over on weekends. It all sounded logical, although rather idyllic, and I was convinced that we were on the road to parental bliss.

If pregnancy was an indication of the joys to come, I was sold. For the most part it was uneventful, even enjoyable, and I looked forward to the birth of our first child. But the night my water broke, my eagerness started to turn to anxiety. On the way to the hospital, I began to think about the awesome responsibility of having a child. The idea of having almost complete control over another person was scary and grew scarier with each contraction. I had read books and articles on the subject of parenting, but I lacked any practical experience with babies. I had never held, fed, bathed, or changed a newborn. What business did I have becoming a mother, I thought?

It seemed somehow ironic to me that these fears should surface at such a late date. But caught up in the excitement of my daughter's birth, I tried to momentarily push aside my worries. Weighing in at 8 lbs. 6 ozs. with a full head of hair and a barrel chest, Elizabeth hardly looked like a newborn, and I was glad that she was so big because I was afraid of handling a small baby. Actually, I was afraid of handling a baby of any size, a painful truth that I never admitted to anyone.

When I came home from the hospital, I watched my fears multiply daily. I worried the baby wouldn't eat or sleep enough or that she would eat or sleep too much, that she might be too cold or too warm. When visitors came, I worried that her schedule would be upset or that she might catch a cold from their children. When her grandparents arrived to see their first grandchild, I stewed over their well-intentioned but overeager advice. I began to feel that motherhood was an overwhelming burden. It seemed that other mothers enjoyed their babies, while I spent most of my time worrying. Each day grew longer as Elizabeth grew more demanding.

Then one day I watched some neighborhood preschoolers romping outside my window. Sometimes they would stumble and cry; other times they would fight and cry. But they would always brush themselves off and continue playing. They were surviving the pitfalls of toddlerhood and enjoying themselves.

At one point a mother came out to rescue her crying daughter, who had stumbled down the front porch steps. As I watched the mother calmly help her daughter up and soothe her with a pat on the back, I thought how nonchalantly she had dealt with the situation. I probably would have carried Elizabeth into the house, checking and rechecking for serious injury. As if in response to her mother, the little girl resumed playing with the others and was soon immersed in a new game.

Not long after, an aggressive little girl pushed another on to the sidewalk in a struggle over a favorite toy. Her mother reprimanded her daughter for this action, while the other child's mother threw her arms around her child and angrily demanded that the aggressive child leave. The "victim," who had not been crying, burst into tears and clung to her mother. Following suit, the aggressor began to cry. When both mothers and daughters left angrily, I had to admit to amusement and more than mild guilt over what my reaction to the situation probably would have been.

By overreacting, one mother alienated another mother and daughter, separated her own child from play with others, and had reinforced her child's dependence on her.

This was only one instance, but I saw how it could affect a mother-child relationship. More important, I saw how perfectly it mirrored my relationship with Elizabeth.

The more I showed my fear of her encountering obstacles, the less likely she was to surmount them. I was not pleased with my thoughts or with our relationship, which didn't seem to be doing either of us much good. I stopped to think about what I really wanted for Elizabeth, and it didn't take long for me to realize that I wanted her to be one of the "toddler survivors," to brush herself off and keep going when she encountered obstacles in childhood and adulthood relationships. I would make a serious mistake if I tried to survive for her, and I resolved to control my overprotectiveness.

Since I had become totally wrapped up in her care, my first step was to occupy myself with something other than Elizabeth. I began leaving her with a baby-sitter for a few hours at a time, and although I worried initially, I was rewarded on my return to find her absorbed in some activity.

I went to museums and shopping malls. Through my church I became a volunteer for the elderly. I renewed friendships with old friends and occasionally went out to lunch. I took up jogging, went on nature hikes, walked around the block, and joined the YWCA. I started playing the piano again and painting with water colors. Best of all, I spent some long overdue time talking with my husband, getting to know him all over again. Gradually, it became easier to take on more activities, and my husband began to take over some of Elizabeth's care.

Although we had agreed initially that he would do this, I never allowed him much time in Elizabeth's routine care. I guess I never really trusted him or thought that he could do the job as well as I could. He can't, but it doesn't really matter. He doesn't feed her like I do, her diapers barely stay up, her clothing never quite suits conditions, and naptime is seldom constant, but the baby loves him and the time they spend together. Daddy has become special to her, and the break from routine helps all of us adjust to our new world.

Elizabeth continues to prosper and has become much more interested in exploring her surroundings and less interested in hanging on to me. She seems so much more active and curious. My husband and I both enjoy her antics and our relationship with her, and motherhood no longer looms ominously on the horizon. It hasn't been easy, but I am making headway. When the urge to worry strikes, I try to do something constructive, until I can face the worry rationally. I love my daughter, I hope, too much to smother her. I owe that much to my baby, and Elizabeth and I are both much happier. □

THE SMALL CRISIS

By Sheila Shafer

"When you've known a child for nearly two years, it's fairly easy to tell whether he's being manipulative or sincere, and in this case Jed appeared to be genuinely frightened."

I've never been at ease with the unexpected, so during my first pregnancy, I used the nine months to take a kind of crash course in what I might look forward to in my new role as a mother. I devoured all the baby care books and articles I could get my hands on. I solicited advice from friends of mine with children, had long discussions with my husband, and even attempted to draw on my own experiences as an elementary school teacher, to extrapolate backwards, as it were, from a part-time responsibility for 35 children to a full-time responsibility for one. When zero hour arrived, I had the rather smug impression that I had sufficiently prepared myself to deal with whatever a child might bring into our lives.

My naiveté was short-lived. I had not been a mother very long before I realized that children are unpredictable, special cases every one, and that no amount of boning up beforehand will eliminate the surprises they bring with them. Though my husband and I managed to move successfully through such critical times as weaning, toilet training, and colic, by combining my "book learning" with a little ingenuity of our own, we often found ourselves faced with situations unique to our child and our family. I think that it was through these situations, when we were "on our own" and unable to draw on anyone else's experiences or observations, that we finally became aware of the full implication and real challenge of being parents.

One such case stands out memorably in my recollections of our son's early childhood.

Jed was just approaching two when he went through what I called—for lack of any official label—his "Isolation Crisis." It came at a time that I think must be particularly difficult for children—that time when a child moves away from the absolute security of being a baby toward the unknown role of toddler. Jed had by the age of twenty months quite mastered walking and running, had acquired a vocabulary he seemed satisfied with, had long since been weaned, and was toilet trained throughout the day, nearly ready to abandon the one diaper at night. In short, he was becoming an independent being. All seemed to be going well, and my husband and I were greatly satisfied, if somewhat overwhelmed, by this "new person" in our house. And then suddenly something went a little wrong.

It happened one evening while the three of us were eating dinner. Jed had taken scarcely two bites of his meal when he put down his fork and pointed to his father and said, "Daddy." We replied, "Yes," and began to eat again, when he pointed to himself and said, "Daddy?" We said, "No, you're Jed." With that his bottom lip began to quiver, the unmistakable sign of tears. Instead of crying, though, he gathered himself together and went through the same procedure with me. "Mama?" he asked, again pointing to himself. "No baby, you're Jed." With that the flood of tears was unleashed and dinner was forgotten as my husband and I, attempted to solace, by now, a nearly hysterical child.

The next night as we began to seat ourselves around the dinner table, Jed refused his highchair and climbed instead onto his father's lap, and with his lower lip quivering again said, "Daddy-me." It was a phrase we were to hear often in the next two weeks. He ate his dinner with his father, on his father's lap and off his father's plate, that night and for nearly a week to come. Whenever we attempted to put him in his own chair, he began a kind of panicked crying. When you've known a child for nearly two years, it's fairly easy to tell whether he's being manipulative or sincere, and in this case Jed appeared to be genuinely frightened. Though neither of us had ever read anywhere that allowing your child to sit on your lap while eating dinner was a valid solution to anything, we decided that given the circumstances, this was our only choice.

In the two weeks following that initial dinnertime disturbance, our child changed from a seemingly secure, outgoing individual into a clinger, a crier, and a lap-sitter. Bedtime, never particularly easy in our house, now became impossible. It was necessary for either my husband or me to sit by Jed's bed for almost three hours until he was asleep, and his last words before sleep were usually, "Daddy-me" or "Jed is Mama."

As in previous crises, we reached for Dr. Spock's dependable *Baby and Child Care,* and while Jed had some of the symptoms of the two-year-old's "fear of separation," we did not feel that this was the real problem. He had rarely been left in the care of anyone other than us, and we had not moved or made any significant changes in our routine. We therefore felt that Jed's fears originated with *him* rather than having been stimulated by something in his environment. These fears, only too real to him, seemed to center around his desire to be either his father or his mother, rather than the separate entity that was himself.

Since I was the parent who spent the most time with our child, I put a great deal of energy into attempting to understand and work through this unhappy phase. I remembered reading somewhere an article by an anthropologist who compared the maturing of a child to the evolution of man as a species. Jed's difficulty set me to thinking about this article, and I began to wonder if at some point in the development of man's brain there came a moment when he became suddenly conscious of the fact that he was *not* the cave that sheltered him, *not* the trees that offered him escape from his enemies, *not* the animals he slew for food, *not even* the mate he lay with or the children that ensued from that relationship, but rather a thing apart, a being utterly.

I suspect most of us have had occasion to realize the separateness of the individual from all and everyone that surrounds him. In times of trouble, great loss, or emotional pain, it becomes obvious that despite sympathetic friends, a supportive family, and an understanding mate, the only person who can *really* deal with your private pain is you. This realization is a giant step toward becoming a whole, healthy, and productive individual, but it is also a kind of sobering and lonely thought. I began wondering if Jed, taking these first uncertain steps toward independence, had come to some similar conclusion of his own.

For the first time in his life, he could move about freely on his own, no longer reliant on us as his sole means of transportation. Now, because of his mastery of fork and spoon and agile fingers, he depended on us only to supply his food rather than, by breast or bottle, make sure it reached its destination. He was also becoming aware of his bodily functions, and he knew that he was the only one who could control his wetting or bowel movements. His newfound ability to talk must have been still another clue to his separateness from us.

The more my husband and I examined the evidence, the more we were convinced that Jed had, in fact, come to the new and frightening conclusion that he was unique and separate from the two individuals who until only recently he had depended upon for his very existence. We never felt that this amateur theory of ours contradicted Spock's sensitive discussion of the two-year-old's "fear of separation," but rather that it enforced it. After all, a child cannot fear separation from his parents until he *realizes* that his physical and mental isolation from them makes that separation a rather terrifying possibility.

We dealt with Jed's problem somewhat stumblingly at first, and then as we began to sense the origin of his fears, with something approaching confidence. Our first rule of thumb was to take Jed's fears seriously. Though we initially had no idea what was causing his tears, it was obvious that they were real and that the only way to stop their constant flow was to spend a good portion of the day holding, cuddling, soothing, and reassuring him.

Perhaps we took this sudden change in our child too seriously, for we had barely warmed to the task of dealing with it when it seemed to disappear altogether. Jed's appetite reappeared, outdoors was the only place he wanted to be, and he became once again so self-absorbed that we were hard put to coax him onto our laps. He was off into new business as though the worrisome two weeks had never happened. We were, of course, relieved and even wondered to ourselves if our theory was correct and our solutions really necessary. What had actually been going on in his head was something only Jed, the unique and separate person that he was, knew.

Our theories were unimportant; the fatigue and confusion were forgotten. What did count was that the three of us had survived some difficult moments together and that moving successfully through this particular challenge, we were left with a heightened and satisfying sense of what it meant to be a family. □

CHAPTER 5

STORIES ABOUT CHILDREN WITH SPECIAL NEEDS

BEING A SPECIAL MOTHER

By Natalie Cinelli

"I would actually pray that when I went to my daughter's crib in the morning, I would find a normal, healthy, bouncing baby waiting for me. Imagine the hurt and disappointment and even the anger I felt each time when my baby's imperfections were still there."

When my daughter was born, the doctor told me I had given birth to a boy. So severe were our baby's abnormalities that it was not until the next day, after a chromosome test, that my husband and I knew that, in fact, we were the parents of a baby girl. A very special baby. A baby, perfect in all ways from the waist up, but with multiple defects in her lower body. Stephanie was born with her intestines literally spilling out of her, with spinal cord damage and clubbed feet, a defective bladder, and no genitals. She is indeed a very special little girl.

How did I react to the news that our baby was not perfect? I was shattered, of course. There had been no warning during the nine months of a seemingly normal pregnancy that anything was wrong. I had not been sick, I had not taken any medication—not even an aspirin—nor did I smoke or take more than a social drink. The fact that this happened for no apparent reason made it that much harder to accept. The doctors could give us no explanation. It just seemed so unfair.

What did it feel like to be thrust suddenly into the role of mother of a handicapped child? There were feelings of anger, bitterness, resentment, helplessness, and overwhelming grief. Especially the first year. I could not take Stephanie home with me from the hospital as other mothers do and as I had done with my firstborn, Matthew. She had been rushed immediately after her birth to another hospital for emergency surgery, and she remained there in the pediatric intensive care unit for six weeks before we took her home for the first time.

During those weeks I experienced none of the joy that a mother is supposed to feel for her newborn. There had not been the usual bonding between mother and child. I didn't actually hold my daughter in my arms until several weeks after she was born. Instead of joy, I felt sorrow and pain every time I visited her in the hospital and saw my tiny infant wrapped in bandages with tubes poked into her nose and IVs inserted into her arms and scalp. And, of course, I was envious of every other mother I saw with a healthy baby. Seeing pregnant women in the supermarket or on the street was no easier. I would wish that I were pregnant—starting all over again expecting a healthy baby.

Stephanie was in and out of the hospital several times during her first year of life. Once or twice during critical periods, the doctors told us she might not survive. And I found myself wishing that she would die. How much easier it would be if she did. But mothers aren't supposed to wish their children dead, so I would end up feeling terribly guilty for even thinking such a thing. Now I know that other mothers of handicapped children have expressed the same wish, but for me, at that time, it was just another emotional burden to bear.

So how does a mother of a handicapped child handle these feelings? How does she cope? During these past three years, I have found that there is no magic formula, no easy way out. But there are positive steps a mother can take to help herself in this situation. Perhaps my experiences might also help other mothers of special children.

Accept the fact that your child is indeed handicapped. Do not expect miracles. I wasted myself emotionally thinking of what might have been. I would actually pray that when I went to my daughter's crib in the morning, I would find a normal, healthy, bouncing baby waiting for me. Imagine the hurt and disappointment and even the anger I felt each time when my baby's imperfections were still there. It took me a long time to realize how silly it was to expose myself to such pain. But gradually, however, I began to see how much better it was for me and for Stephanie if I could accept her and love her as she was, not as I would want her to be. Today I am thankful that she is the bright, happy, loving child that she is. In other words, adopt a more realistic attitude rather than wasting time on delusions and wishful thinking.

Reach out for help. It is so very easy for the mother of a handicapped child to fall into the trap of self-pity. Instead of becoming a martyr, welcome all the help there is available to you.

There were times during Stephanie's infancy that I truly believed only I was capable of caring for her. After all, she was no ordinary baby and so she required extraordinary care, I thought. The result, of course, was that I felt completely overburdened by the day-to-day routine of taking care of my baby. In my mind there was no escape. I was trapped at home with a three-year-old toddler and a very unusual infant who could not be left in the hands of the usual baby-sitter.

Time and experience have shown me how wrong I was. Fortunately, it didn't take me too long to realize that my husband was just as good, if not in some ways better, with Stephanie as I was. There is a natural affinity between fathers and daughters anyway, and Stephanie and her daddy have that special relationship. So my husband could baby-sit and leave me free to spend time by myself or alone with my son.

On occasion we also used the services of a visiting nurse or a student nurse. The hospital made the initial arrangements for a visiting nurse for Stephanie. Even if the nurse came just once a week to look in on her, it was reassuring to me to hear someone say that everything was just fine and that I was doing a good job. However, as Stephanie has grown older, I feel just as comfortable leaving her with a regular baby-sitter or a friend or her grandparents.

Stephanie has also started going to nursery school. It is important for the parents of the handicapped to know that in most cases education is available and must be provided for their child. But you must reach out for it.

Proceed with your normal family life. Don't alter your lifestyle because of your special child. This would not be fair to you and your husband and to your other children, or in fact, to the handicapped child herself. Do not make unnecessary concessions "for the sake of the baby." Instead, include her in as many family activities as possible. And never make the mistake of pampering or spoiling your child because she is handicapped.

From the very beginning my husband and I decided that Stephanie's physical problems were simply inconveniences and not obstacles in her life. As a result, she has accompanied us on plane trips and automobile rides, and she is quite at home whether in a motel or friend's house, in a restaurant or at a backyard barbeque.

Join a group of parents or mothers with handicapped children. It is only in the past few months that my husband and I finally became members of the Massachusetts Spina Bifida Association. Although various people had suggested we look into this soon after Stephanie was born, I just didn't want to be categorized, I guess, as the mother of a handicapped child. Now that we are members, I can see how much we've missed — not only the advice and support of other parents but also useful information and relevant medical news.

I'm also involved in the mothers' group at the school that Stephanie attends. Once a week we sit and talk over coffee with the school social worker. We share our thoughts and feelings and offer each other a listening ear whenever there is a problem. But most important to me is the knowledge that I am not alone.

I am just one of the many mothers of special children. I like to believe that we are special too.   □

BORN WITH A CLEFT PALATE

By Carol L. Hunter

"By the next day the numbing effect of the 'miracle of birth' had worn off, and the shock of reality hit us full force. Our child was not normal."

Mine was a perfect pregnancy. I never felt happier or looked better in my life. My complexion was clear, my hair was shiny, and I glowed with that special excitement that comes from anticipating the birth of a first child.

My husband, Steve, and I had taken the six-week Lamaze course together so that he could be with me throughout labor and delivery. Steve turned out to be a terrific coach, and labor went smoothly. Most of my four hours in the labor room were spent watching television soap operas and eating jello. When the contractions started to get fairly intense, everything began moving so quickly that I was in the delivery room before I knew it. Steve was snapping pictures of me as if I were a marathon runner crossing the finish line, and on the third push our baby daughter was forced out into the world.

No matter how many millions of times this drama had been played before, we still felt like the first people on earth to have participated in the miracle of birth. Steve and I felt so incredibly exhilarated that we barely heard the doctor when he said solemnly and tenuously, "We have a little problem here." I wasn't sure whether he was talking to us or to the nurses, but within seconds he came around the delivery table to my side and asked, "Do you know what a cleft palate is?"

I knew. I had majored in communications in college and had taken one speech course in which cleft lip and palate were discussed as part of a unit on speech handicaps, but I remembered almost nothing about it. I listened in a fog as the doctor explained that our little girl had been born with a cleft of her lip and palate.

As I look back on that moment, I don't recall if we even reacted. Having my husband at my side during the delivery made the news that our baby was born less than perfect somehow easier to accept. We greeted our daughter with the same love and enthusiasm that any new parents feel when they first hold that soft, warm bundle. Perhaps it was our unbridled joy at finally being a family that allowed Steve and me to calmly wait for the pediatrician who had been called in to talk to us.

We had never met Dr. Lefrak before that day, but this first meeting with him told us we had made a good choice. He was understanding, sympathetic, and knowledgeable.

Dr. Lefrak began the conversation by telling us that he had just examined Shari and found everything else to be normal. Steve and I were very relieved. We were later to learn that one out of every six cleft lip children has at least one other birth defect as well, ranging from joined-together toes, malformed ears, spina bifida, congenital heart disease, and clubfoot, to the absence of genitals. According to some studies the percentage of cleft lip children with associated abnormalities may be as high as 51 percent. Shari had been lucky.

We listened attentively as our doctor explained exactly what cleft lip and cleft palate are. The face of the infant, he told us, begins to develop at approximately seven to nine weeks after conception. Gradually two horseshoe-shaped swellings appear on either side of the midline of the face and slowly move toward each other to form the nostrils. Other bulges of tissue just below grow toward the midline to meet the tips of the nasal swellings to form the completed upper lip. The gap between these lumps of tissue should fuse by the end of the second month of development to form a completed upper lip all in one piece. When fusion does not take place or is not completed, an open gap results, which we call a cleft lip. The extent of the cleft can vary from a slight notching of the red portion of the lip to a total separation of the lip into two or three sections. In our daughter's case the nostrils were not completely formed, and a central section of lip and bone hung down with a large opening on either side.

Since the face is not formed all in one piece at the start, neither is the roof of the mouth. The palate forms from the sides of the upper jaw, which grow toward the middle of the mouth and fuse by the end of the third month. If there is any interference with initial fusion of the sides of the jaw, the baby is born with a cleft extending the entire length of the palate. If part of the fusion is accomplished before the interference occurs, the child is born with a partial cleft of the palate. Dr. Lefrak told us that Shari's cleft was the most serious kind, extending from the soft palate, the back part of the roof of the mouth composed largely of muscle that moves upward and backward in the process of speech and swallowing, into the front of the mouth, leaving an opening in the hard palate, the bony front part of the roof of the mouth.

"How could this have happened?" I asked. "My pregnancy was perfect. There never was any hint of a problem."

The pediatrician had no answers. Approximately one of every 675 infants is born with a problem like Shari's. Cleft defects are the most common serious birth defect second only to clubfoot, yet very little is known about why they occur. Although heredity seems to play a role in some cases, it is by no means a major or sole cause. We had no history of cleft defect on either side of the family. More interestingly, in studies done on identical twins, where the genetic inheritance is the same, cleft lip occurs only in 40 percent of both children. This would suggest that other influences in the womb may cause a cleft defect in a susceptible infant. Exactly what these influences are remains unknown. I felt better knowing it was nothing I did during my pregnancy that caused Shari's problem.

Later that evening we met with the plastic surgeon called in by Dr. Lefrak, and he confirmed the pediatrician's assurances that although rehabilitation was a long road, we could expect our baby to eventually have a very nearly normal lip and palate. Most plastic surgeons, he told us, operate to correct the lip when the child is about three months old. The palate is usually corrected at about a year and a half. We would have to select a surgeon within the next two months.

Today cleft lip and palate children are generally treated by a cleft palate team, a group of specialists including a pediatrician, plastic surgeon, orthodontist, an otolaryngologist (ear, nose, and throat doctor), a speech pathologist, audiologist, and a social worker who work together to help make the baby into a healthy child. Fortunately, our hospital had such a cleft palate team and served as a valuable resource for us.

The next few days would be a busy whirl of getting to know my new daughter, adjusting emotionally to having a handicapped child, and reading frantically to learn all I could about Shari's birth defect.

The emotional adjustment was no easy matter. By the next day the numbing effect of the "miracle of birth" had worn off, and the shock of reality hit us full force. Our child was not normal. So many of my expectations would have to be abandoned. For so long I had looked forward to nursing my baby. That idea had to be given up because Shari's cleft made normal sucking impossible. I fed her not in my room but in the nursery, where I was taught how to hold the baby and the bottle so she would get enough to eat. Most cleft palate children must be fed with a special cleft palate feeder, bubble syringe, or medicine dropper, but luckily Shari was able to use a regular bottle fit with a special nipple. Still, she took very little milk at each feeding, chewing on the nipple rather than actually sucking. When I finally got her home, feeding would be an all-day affair with one mealtime sliding into the next because formula was taken so slowly.

I had always taken for granted that my baby would be beautiful, but now that deformed mouth and nose made it impossible to picture Shari's ever looking pretty despite her big, blue, saucer-shaped eyes; small, flat ears; perfectly formed head, covered by thick, black hair; and her flawless, milky complexion. What would she look like after plastic surgery? All I could imagine was the typical "hare-lip" I had seen sometime in the past—a prominent scar, misshapen or raised at the center. At least a man could grow a mustache to cover the upper lip, but how could my little girl ever hide the deformity? Would children make fun of her? Would Shari suffer the cleft palate complications I had read about such as hearing loss or speech defect? In those first days following Shari's birth, we were overwhelmed by worry.

The day following delivery, I was visited by the hospital social worker. It had been at her suggestion and urging that a cleft palate parents' group had been set up under hospital auspices just one year before our daughter's birth. The group began as a small collection of parents who thought it might be helpful to share their experiences and talk to one another about the problems, both major and minor, of raising their special child. Once-a-month meetings were held, and by a wonderful coincidence such a meeting was scheduled this night, just a little more than 24 hours after Shari's birth, when we needed support and information the most.

Steve attended the meeting without me, as I was not yet permitted to leave the maternity floor. He returned later that evening laden with reading material and brimming with enthusiasm and new hope. Other parents had spoken candidly with him, reassuring him that our newborn would be a healthy, normal child. The parents of older children proudly showed him pictures of their beautiful sons and daughters who had already been through corrective surgery. That night a local plastic surgeon gave a lecture on cleft palate and lip surgery, explaining how it is generally done and showing slides that emphasized the marvelous results of modern plastic surgery in these cases. Steve's hopefulness was contagious, and I began to believe that Shari would be all right.

When we took Shari home, the help and support of the parents' group followed us. The social worker or one of the parents was always available to answer my questions about Shari's care or provide feeding equipment or help me keep the faith that Shari's problem would be corrected in time. Yet it was difficult to be denied the pleasure of showing off my baby to neighbors on our daily walks, and there was still a gnawing uncertainty about so many things. What plastic surgeon would we decide to use, and would Shari ever be really normal?

Choosing a surgeon was not easy. We went for many consultations in and out of state. Each doctor had a slightly different methodology and surgical timetable. Some would do the lip in two stages and the palate in one stage; others advocated one lip surgery and two operations on the palate; some opted for still another procedure. When we finally decided on a plastic surgeon, it was as much an emotional decision as a rational one.

It was a snowy day in December when Sharon Breedlove came to visit me with her beautiful and delightfully normal two-year-old, Melissa. They had moved to Florida a few months earlier and were up north just for a short visit; yet they made the ride out to see us because of a common bond. Melissa had been born with the same birth defect as Shari's. I had never met Sharon or Melissa before, but I will never forget them.

When I looked at Melissa, all I saw was a lovely child. Her happy, bright smile made the slight scar above her lip insignificant, and when she said, "I love you, Mommy," her words were even more treasured for what it had taken to ensure that speech. As I held my two-month-old disfigured baby close to my breast, I looked at the miracle that was Melissa, and I was finally convinced that Shari would make it.

From that day on I had new courage. We decided to use our local surgeon. His former patient Melissa was the only testimonial we needed.

Our decision was the right one. Today Shari has been through three operations. Her lip looks quite normal, and she has an adorable button nose. It is impossible for us to remember what she looked like before surgery; although we can still recall with laughter the way she used to smile from ear to ear, literally, before her lip was closed and how, much to our embarrassed horror, she would stick her little finger up through her open palate and out her nose to wave. She is still a very special child to us but because of her abilities and not her inabilities. Shari began speaking at fifteen months, well before her palate was closed, and we appear to have avoided all those complications I feared so much. No one seems to notice her little scar, only her beautiful smile.

I can't imagine what it would have been like to have had a normal child and not to have gone through the trauma of Shari's birth defect. I believe, though, that there is a purpose in all things, and Shari's problems made us more acutely aware of her blessings. Her defects made us more appreciative of her strengths. No advance she made went unnoticed no matter how small; no new word went uncheered. □

FINDING OUT ABOUT MY BABY'S HEART MURMUR

By Suzanne Perry

"'What are you afraid of?' I asked myself. I suppose any loving parent could guess my answer. I was afraid of losing my baby."

"**S**he's healthy and alert. She seems to be gaining well..."

I relaxed back on the pillow in my hospital room, listening with a grin as the doctor enumerated all the superior qualities of our new baby daughter. She was the product of a healthy and much wanted pregnancy. She had had a normal, unmedicated birth with her daddy on hand to help bring her into the world. Certainly she was perfect.

"...and she had an Apgar score of 9. But there is just one thing.'"

I froze.

"She does have a heart murmur."

Heart murmur! What does a heart murmer indicate? How will it affect her? Dozens of questions flashed through my mind. But before any of them could be voiced, I felt my eyes fill with tears, and then no sound came out at all.

"...a tightening of the pulmonic valve of a ventricular septal defect," he was continuing. "It's just very difficult to tell on babies this small."

"Will she be all right?" I finally mustered.

He looked uncomfortable. "Well, we'll follow it. Bring her in to my office in three weeks, and we'll listen again." And then he was gone.

By this time I was openly weeping—deep, wracking, frightened sobs. When my husband, Deane, called a few minutes later, I tearfully told him about the baby's murmur, and he shared my grief and confusion.

Somehow, though, life seems to be a constant process of "finding out." After learning of our little girl's condition, it seemed only logical to find out all we could. By the time we appeared at the doctor's office three weeks later, we had done our homework.

We stood by, silent and tense, as he placed the stethoscope on her chest. We could tell by the look on his face before he said a word that the murmur was still there. However, we were comforted by our new knowledge that today so many heart problems that would have been considered serious or even fatal in our parents' day can now be completely corrected. We had also discovered that some murmurs, sometimes called functional murmurs, occur from time to time in children and are of no significance at all.

Unfortunately, our daughter's murmur didn't fall into the functional category, and we were sent to specialists to determine its cause.

The diagnosis was finally in. Gena had "Patent Ductus Arteriosis." Everyone assured us that if you have a heart problem, this is the one to have. At first this seemed small comfort.

However, as we continued our research, we learned that we were indeed fortunate. Not only was this relatively common problem the earliest heart abnormality to be successfully operated on, but also it would not require "open heart" surgery, in which the heart mechanism is stopped. But two surgical procedures would be required.

During the three weeks preceding the surgery, I became increasingly tense. At first I couldn't figure out why. I had "found out" everything there was to know about the actual procedures, the hospital routine, and any possible complications. But throughout my investigation, the one question I had failed to ask was, "How do I feel about all of this?"

As I forced myself to take a good look at this, I saw that primary among my feelings was fear. "What are you afraid of?" I asked myself. I suppose any loving parent could guess my answer. I was afraid of losing my baby.

The cardiologist had been straight with us. I knew that there was less than one chance in a hundred that she would die and that the benefits far outweighed the risks of the operation, but as he told us, there is always the possibility of an "accident."

My husband and I sat down that evening and did some sharing. We talked about all of the fears that we had each been carrying around within ourselves while trying to be brave for the other person. We discovered that our biggest fear was of having to come home without her.

By the time Gena went into the hospital, we were ready. Certainly the days of her stay in the hospital were the longest and toughest days of our entire lives, but our preparation made all the difference.

Gena's surgery went smoothly and well. Still, we hardly recognized the pale little ghost that emerged from the operating room. She was hooked up with so many tubes and wires. When we followed her up to intensive care and found out what each tube and wire was for and how each functioned to protect her, we felt a lot more comfortable and relieved.

As I write this, it is exactly one month after Gena's operation. If you couldn't see the scars from her incisions, which incidentally grow fainter every day, you would never know that she had undergone major surgery. We have seen great gains in her appetite, energy, and development just in these past few weeks. It makes every second of those difficult days seem well worthwhile to see Gena shrieking with laughter as she speeds across the floor with a fast crawl.

We intend to continue our policy of "finding out" as we confront each new challenge in Gena's life and our own. "Finding out" can be the best medicine for everyone concerned. □

HE'S DEAF

By Judy McLaughlin

"...the audiologist explained that he'd had a hard time determining the degree of Shaun's deafness because of his age. But he felt Shaun was somewhere in the profound range."

It was a sunny spring day in Nevada. My one-year-old son, Shaun, was crawling around our mobile home, investigating as usual, and I was busy cooking, cleaning, and talking on the phone to my friends.

But today when one of my girl friends called, she hinted that she had something serious to discuss with me. A group of other mothers at church had decided that since she knew me best, she should be the one to tell me. They all felt there might be a problem with Shaun. He did not turn to me when called as their children did. Maybe I should have his hearing tested, they wondered, but they didn't want to offend me. I laughed at her suggestion, remarking that their observation didn't bother me a bit. I reminded her that Shaun was more obedient than their children when told to leave things alone. And besides, he always seemed to turn to me when I called him at home. He also came crawling from wherever he was was when I started playing the piano. I was sure there was nothing wrong with his hearing. I tried to be nonchalant about the matter.

That night, however, in mentioning the conversation to my husband, I was not so nonchalant. I remembered how, for the past month, he had been wondering why Shaun hadn't yet said "da-da." Shaun made noise, but not as much as the other babies. My husband didn't want to believe Shaun was deaf either. But keeping our fears to ourselves, we started testing him at home for the next couple of weeks. For example, we would hit a pan while standing behind him or call his name. We'd be sure his attention was on something else while we experimented. Sometimes he would turn, and it really seemed he had heard, but too many times he didn't.

We finally had to admit that Shaun needed professional testing. It happened one morning when I was entering our bedroom and my husband told me to stop. He had Shaun positioned on the bed so he could not see me.

"Now," he said, "call Shaun."

I called. Nothing. I screamed. Nothing. Finally, he pointed and motioned to Shaun with his head in my direction. Shaun turned around and saw me and reached up to me with waiting arms. That day I made an appointment with the state speech and hearing clinic.

My hopes were that he would only be hard-of-hearing. My mother, a teacher in a nearby grade school, had such a pupil in her sixth grade class. The girl had sufficient hearing to have less trouble learning to talk using a hearing aid, than the profoundly or severely deaf children.

The day finally arrived that was to push us into the reality of a whole new world. The audiologist tested Shaun for about 45 minutes. In the soundproof room, Shaun kept looking up and waving. When we sat down to discuss his conclusions, the audiologist explained that he'd had a hard time determining the degree of Shaun's deafness because of his age. But he felt Shaun was somewhere in the profound range.

As I drove home that afternoon, I couldn't keep back the tears. The remaining conversation with the audiologist kept running through my mind. Had Shaun ever been really sick with a high fever? Had I had a normal delivery with him? And so on. Nothing I could recall was abnormal. He was just one of those children who was born deaf.

Recalling the past year of his life, I realized how easily I had missed seeing the signs of his deafness. And I believed part of that was because we lived in a trailer. A trailer is very conducive to vibration, so when Shaun was getting into something he shouldn't, it was very easy to kick the floor to get his attention and tell him "no." After a while he would turn just as I said "no," so it seemed as if he heard me. If he got into things that were permitted, I never took notice, and he usually didn't turn.

It seemed as if he heard the dog pass by my feet while I was nursing him because he would turn over and look down. But, in fact, he was watching my eyes, and as the dog passed, I'd speak out to her or follow her with my eyes. He would see my attention on something below him and turn to look. He would come from another room when I played the piano because of the deep vibrations *felt,* not heard.

I was told of a program for handicapped children at a nearby university. I took Shaun that summer, but I was dissatisfied because the things they suggested were things I had already done. It turned out that the program was mostly for the multihandicapped and not specifically suited for the deaf. I couldn't do anything with the school for the deaf because they were closed for the summer, so I worked on sign language with Shaun and put off school in the fall because I did not know they had a parent-infant program.

Finally in October, at the insistent urging of a friend, I went to investigate the program. I enrolled my son in the parent-infant training program, which is set up to train both the parent and child in total language skills for the deaf. Shaun went once a week for training that first year. The next year his teacher came to our home once a week, since I no longer owned a car.

A local elementary school had a program for preschoolers, and I chose a program for Shaun that is set up to train the child and parent with a sign language. I chose this because, for a profoundly deaf child, life gets pretty frustrating if just oral skills are taught.

Recent studies are showing that even with handicapped children, the best learning environment is in the home under the mother's care. Dr. Raymond S. Moore, author of the book *Better Late Than Early*, says that with the aid of outside learning materials for the mother's use in education, the home is a better environment for gaining the child's confidence.

We believe in this philosophy and have tried to give Shaun every opportunity for learning at home. He now has a personal usage vocabulary of about 150 words in sign language but understands about 100 more than that. He does not sign complete sentences yet himself, but he tries. He usually asks for the sign of something new if he does not know it. He can say "mama" and "ball" because these are visual words, but it will take much longer to train him to speak the whole English language. He has already tried to teach his five-month-old sister some sign language. He recently tried to get her to sign "mama" and "father." When she didn't do it, he took her tiny hand and did it with her.

Deafness is the silent, hard-to-detect handicap. I suggest that every parent of every newborn insist that a startle test be given. It doesn't hurt to check every few months to ensure that the child is hearing normally.

Sometimes a child's deafness is due only to a blockage and can be corrected with a tube inserted in the canal. Sometimes a child is only hard-of-hearing and can hear almost normally with the use of hearing aids. But if severe nerve damage is the cause, hearing aids will only aid in learning to speak by using what small amount of hearing the child has. But time is important, so the sooner the parent discovers deafness, the better.

It is very hard for most people to realize that Shaun is deaf. He appears quite normal. He's a whiz visually. Someday, I suspect, he will be a top ballplayer. He has an aim you can't believe for a two-year-old. He is very sociable and loves to be with other children. He will be somewhat behind for a few years academically, but when he reaches adulthood, if he can overcome his handicap as well as he has been doing so far and not let it overcome him, he will be richly blessed in understanding and helping others. □

LIVING WITH A LEARNING DISABLED CHILD

By Harriet Fein

"I was determined that in order to live with myself, I had to try every avenue I could to give Larry a 'normal' life regardless of the financial, physical, or emotional cost I'd pay; if not, my conscience would forever be in turmoil."

In all my years of teaching, I never even knew a child with a learning disability. How could I be the mother of one? Driving home from Newington Children's Hospital, I asked myself this question over and over again. Although it had taken years to identify the root of Larry's different behavior, now that the behavior had a label, I had a mental block against the words "learning disability." Through streaming tears, I kept repeating, "This couldn't be my child they were discussing! I don't understand it!" Truthfully, I really did comprehend the diagnosis; however, I wasn't ready to cope with the reality of the situation.

My problem, not Larry's, was that my expectations about pregnancy and motherhood were assimilated from the smiling faces of babies and mothers on magazine covers. I envisioned my baby as a rosy, beautiful, and serene infant whom I could cater to with endless love and affection. In return this baby would be totally content with all my unselfish devotion. I never really doubted that this would be my situation—until Larry was born and my fantasy collapsed.

Larry created havoc from day one! The nurses couldn't stop complaining about his endless screaming. My elation in the new role of motherhood and the flattering attention of all my friends obliterated the nurse's credibility. It was inconceivable to me that I could produce a disruptive child. It was not until we arrived home that I began to wonder what I could possibly do to quiet this distraught, nervous infant.

Our garden apartment echoed Larry's shrill cries night and day. I was constantly apologizing to my neighbors because Larry disrupted their sleep. Larry rarely slept; he constantly kicked, screamed, and turned. My sleep was erratic, and I became overwrought from the continual crying. I kept wondering what I was doing wrong and why this baby was so different. During those first few months, my only escape was to leave the house for a few hours. I couldn't accept that my life had changed so radically and so quickly, and what I had anticipated as the most fulfilling role in my life had turned into an endless nightmare.

During one of Larry's periodic checkups, I questioned the pediatrician about the possibility of Larry's being hyperactive. I had to understand why Larry regurgitated formula, why he couldn't be still, and why he always cried. The pediatrician condescendingly replied, "Mrs. Fein, you don't even know what hyperactive really means." I left his office upset with myself for even asking such a dumb question. After all, an experienced doctor would recognize hyperactivity, so I must be an overreactive, overly concerned mother. I blamed myself for my inadequacy and inexperience as a new mother. Most of all, I felt angry with myself, my child, and the pediatrician.

During the toddler stage Larry turned into my shadow—always behind me and constantly moving. Because his attention span was limited, *Sesame Street, Mister Rogers,* baby swings, toys, and trucks all failed to amuse him. For his own safety, I had to lock cabinets, remove ashtrays, and bolt doors. Larry's exploratory adventures led him to climb refrigerators, mount the stove, and flush anything he could find down the toilet. I just waited for him to become exhausted so I could have some time to be alone or with my husband. It never happened.

When Charlene was born, I was freed from the burden of guilt that I had been feeling for several years. Charlene was a lovable, serene baby who could be caressed and loved without recoiling or crying. Whenever Larry and Charlene were together, I nervously watched their interactions. It wasn't until Charlene was a toddler and could play with Larry that I noticed a change in their relationship. Charlene's gentlest touch could often provoke a volley of angry punches from Larry.

Larry's entry into first grade was like watching a latent volcano in the process of violently erupting. All his pent-up anger, frustration, and rage were unleashed by the time he arrived home. Many times these symptoms were manifested as physical ailments—headaches, stomach aches, and assorted pains. When Larry got off the school bus, tension oozed from his entire body. He would slam the door of his room and remain there, refusing to play with any of his friends. On other occasions he could unleash his hostility by banging objects or his body against the walls of his room. This young boy, whom the teacher viewed as a "model" student, was retreating into a private world of inner torment.

I began to consult doctors, psychologists, and teachers in an attempt to understand my son's erratic behavior. The results were futile, and I began to doubt my own convictions. Maybe Larry really was just going through a childhood phase. As much as I wanted to believe it, I couldn't erase Larry's sad eyes and angry, contorted face from my mind. As much as I was in conflict with myself, my husband, my parents, and professional opinions, I felt that I would be giving up on Larry if I stopped searching for an answer. I was determined that in order to live with myself, I had to try every avenue I could to give Larry a "normal" life regardless of the financial, physical, or emotional cost I'd pay; if not, my conscience would forever be in turmoil.

The monotony and frustration of the endless doctor visits began affecting

Larry until one day, he refused to accompany me. "They don't help me anyway; what's the use?" he said. I took his small hand and stared into his dejected face. "We both know you have problems, but in time someone's going to help us. I promise you I'll be with you every step of the way," I told him. That conversation broke down the remaining barriers between us. Larry began to realize I wasn't ashamed of him or his behavior. I explained that although I didn't always like his behavior, I loved him dearly and would do anything to help us both.

Larry was a lucky boy. After being tested at Newington Children's Hospital, a pediatric neurologist diagnosed Larry as a child with borderline perceptual-motor learning disabilities. The neurologist's suspicions were aroused by a simple drawing Larry had made of a clock. The numbers on the clock were all jumbled together in one corner and drawn backwards.

The occupational therapist explained that children such as Larry, with tactile problems, often turn into behavioral problems. She unraveled the mystery of Larry's aversion to being touched by explaining that Larry had difficulty differentiating a pat from a punch. To Larry all touch felt the same, which explained his defensive reactions to his younger sister's pats.

Occupational therapy was Larry's special world where he was treated as a special child. Lonnie, the therapist, and Newington Hospital represented hope to Larry. When we left his weekly sessions, his hostilities seemed to vanish. Therapy enabled him to learn how to control his anger and monitor his anxieties.

Today, Larry is a well-adjusted third grader who owes a debt of gratitude to a dedicated occupational therapist, a competent child psychologist, and committed teachers. From time to time, there are still moments of raging anger, except that today Larry is aware of what is happening to him. He's learned self-control and is not overwhelmed by shifts in his emotions.

When I look at Larry, I no longer recognize the child that used to be there. His movements are now graceful instead of tense and angular. He is agile and has developed into an outstanding athlete. More than that, I see a glow from within. His eyes smile, and he amuses us with his jokes and trite stories. I hear his laughter instead of his tears. Occasionally Larry and I talk about the "other little boy" who used to live with us. The "other boy" is now a memory, but Larry and I still remember him.

My last birthday was the turning point in my relationship with Larry. On his own he selected a ring to give me. He handed me the ring and said, "Thank you for helping me with all those problems. I love you." I started crying and reached out to hug this little boy who had lived for seven years in a world of torment few adults could understand. When I realized that I was holding Larry tightly against me, I started crying even harder. It had taken seven years to be able to love my son in this way and seven years for him to be able to be receptive to my touch. Larry and I had journeyed a long way for him to learn the very simple concept that touching means love. □

OUR GIFT OF GOD

By Cheryl Pricone Wood

"I felt God had challenged our faith and our strength. We were faced with two choices—we could totally reject our imperfect child, or we could take him home and help him to achieve his greatest potential."

"**D**idn't you notice that he doesn't look like either of you?" was our doctor's awkward way of informing us that our perfect newborn son was, well, not *quite* perfect. "We believe he may have Down Syndrome, or Mongolism as it was formerly called...." The high we had felt all day after the birth of our second child came crashing down around us.

The doctor tried his best to be positive and helpful, knowing that none of the information he offered could erase the pain we felt. "They're *so* affectionate," he said optimistically. "They're always coming in with their runny noses and hugging and kissing me."

The feeling of loss was overwhelming. We thought we had given birth to a son that day; instead we had an "it"—one of those strange-looking children who would grow up to walk clumsily between my husband and me, holding our hands. The baby we had birthed and called Matthew, which means "Gift of God," was not at all the child we had imagined. He was someone entirely different, and now our happiness was mingled with tremendous sorrow for our pitiful creation. Perhaps we should change his name, I thought. I couldn't wait for the doctor to leave so that I could stop asking intelligent questions and acting calm. Then I could look into my husband's eyes and express the sadness I thought would last forever.

At twenty-five I was in the low-risk group for having a baby with Down Syndrome, and therefore, I had never even considered the possibility. Besides, I knew God would never saddle me with a "special needs" child since I barely had enough patience to cope with a normal child. Now I would have to become an expert on Down Syndrome, a champion for the cause. My first reaction to the responsibility of this unwanted upheaval in my life was completely selfish—I resented it.

We went home with a baby boy who suckled, slept, cried, and stared at everything and everybody, just like any other baby. We were advised to give Matthew lots of stimulation with color, music, and touch, which is basically what we would have done with a normal baby. We were advised to join a parent support group and enroll Matthew in an infant stimulation program, but I wasn't ready to get so involved. At two weeks old Matt turned from his stomach to his back. He was strong and active; it was hard to believe he had a real problem.

It took three months for me to get up the nerve to contact the director of the local infant stimulation program. Once I did, I found it helpful because it enabled me to talk to people who know a lot about Matthew's condition and about the educational system we would eventually be part of. Children with Down Syndrome enter public school at age three, but as recently as ten years ago, parents of Down Syndrome newborns were urged to institutionalize their infants. The condition was considered hopeless, and well-meaning doctors cautioned parents that raising the child at home would be pointless. Thanks to some of the early pioneers who refused to accept this prognosis for their children, it is now recognized that many of these children are exceptionally loving and responsive. Today there are group homes where adults with Down Syndrome can live independently of their parents; many are capable of holding a normal job.

The counselors at the infant stimulation program also gave me some helpful ideas for stimulating and playing with Matthew, and best of all, they reinforced our feeling that he was doing extremely well. The contrast between our first image of a child with Down Syndrome and the reality of our delightful son Matthew was tremendous. We felt incredibly blessed.

A woman at a party said to me, "I could cope with my child having a physical handicap, but I would not be able to handle a retarded child." But you never know how you will handle what outwardly appears to be a tragedy until you are forced to. I didn't bother to ask, "Why me?" because I knew the answer was, "Why not me?" I did wonder what could have led to the formation of an extra chromosome in our child, but I would not waste energy by feeling guilty. I felt God had challenged our faith and our strength. We were faced with two choices—we could totally reject our imperfect child, or we could take him home and help him to achieve his greatest potential. The choice to love our son was simple. Maybe he never could become a doctor or scientist, but he certainly could become a happy, healthy, functioning human being.

Matthew is two years old now. He is bright, curious, and independent, much like the other two-year-olds that we know. He is also a funny little guy with an irresistible smile. So far, strangers that we meet react so positively to Matthew's charm that it amazes me. My fears that he would be treated like a freak were unfounded; people genuinely think he's cute.

Yes, there are times of sorrow over our son's condition. Right now Matthew is doing above average for a child with Down Syndrome, but certainly there are all sorts of concerns for the future. Most parents worry about their child's future, and having a normal child is no guarantee of happiness. Having a son like Matthew to share life with, regardless of his affliction, is no tragedy. It is a privilege and a joy. □

RAISING A CHILD WITH DOWN SYNDROME

By Teresa Kinman

"I discovered feelings in myself I never knew had existed. My reactions ranged from bitterness to pity for myself and my child."

Having already survived two and a half years with a bright, inquisitive little girl, I looked forward to the birth of my second child with the seasoned confidence of a commanding general. I fully expected this baby to be as much of a challenge as her older sister, and I would welcome every moment of it.

After nine months of a very normal pregnancy, my second little girl was born. Following a Lamaze delivery, my husband and I rejoiced over our beautiful baby girl. Consequently, I was stunned the next morning when our family doctor tried to tell me as gently as he could, "Your baby is a mongoloid." I had no idea what he meant, but I knew it was not good. In that split second it seemed as though my nearly organized life had been shattered.

Through my tears our doctor tried to explain to me exactly what Down Syndrome is. It is a genetic disorder, and there is no explainable cause. There was nothing we could have done to prevent it since it occurred at the moment of conception. Laura was born with 47 chromosomes instead of the usual 46. This caused several results.

Laura's physical appearance varied slightly from the normal newborn's, although this was not evident to a person unfamiliar with Down Syndrome. Her head was slightly smaller, her ears were a little lower set, and her nose was flatter at the bridge, giving her the typical profile of a child with Down Syndrome. Although these physical characteristics are evident to me now, most people looking at Laura thought she was a normal, healthy newborn.

By far the more serious result, however, was that our baby was mentally retarded. Having never been exposed to the mentally handicapped before, I presumed the worst and completely panicked.

In those hours after we were told, my husband, Rod, and I held each other, cried together, and decided as a family we would do everything possible for our little Laura. Families and friends were very supportive and encouraging, and we were both thankful for their presence.

The three days in the hospital following her birth were the most difficult of my life. I discovered feelings in myself I never knew had existed. My reactions ranged from bitterness to pity for myself and my child. There was a child in the nursery with a cleft palate, and I would hear people murmuring about how sad it was for the baby and the parents. I couldn't help but think that although my baby looked normal to them, her problem wasn't correctable by surgery, as that child's was.

The best advice was given to us by our dear family physician, who suggested that we take her home to care for and love, just like any other child. Finally home again, things seemed brighter than before. My two-year-old was there to make me smile, and she was delighted with her new sister. The four of us were united as a family, and it seemed to me that together we could indeed handle anything.

We took positive action to ensure that Laura would have every possible advantage. We are fortunate to live in Omaha, Nebraska, where there is a fine facility for handicapped children. I contacted Meyers Children's Rehabilitation Institute, and by the time Laura was seven weeks old, she was enrolled in their infant stimulation program. This Institute does a fantastic job with the handicapped. The emphasis is put on interaction between parent and child. By attending weekly classes, we have learned the best methods of stimulating Laura through play and exercise. I also have had a chance to observe other children with Down Syndrome, which has been very encouraging to me. The Institute also does a quarterly evaluation of Laura, which lets us know how she is progressing in relation to other children.

We also had a nurse from the visiting nurses association, who came once a month to check on Laura's progress and to supply us with information. My brother-in-law also sent us information from Boston University, which was very encouraging. We realized that the articles which we had previously read were completely outdated. The children we had read about in those books were not fortunate enough to have had the advantages now available to Laura. Twenty years ago, when many of those books were written, many of these children were put in institutions and did not receive the help that is so vital in those early years.

We visited a genetic counselor, who explained Laura's genetic disorder in great detail to us. We were relieved to learn through a chromosome test that Laura's type of Down Syndrome was not inherited. It was a chance event and not likely to happen to us again.

Suddenly it seemed that everyone knew someone who had a child with Down Syndrome. We received countless phone calls from such people, and the reports of these children's progress were definitely encouraging. Best of all was the day-by-day progress of Laura herself. She was not the passive child we had been led to expect. Continually active, she could already roll from her tummy to her back at two weeks. She seemed very much aware of her surroundings and of those who loved her.

We have continued to take her for her weekly stimulation classes because we realize that these first four years are so very important to her learning potential, as indeed they are for every child. We work with her at home, and it is an enjoyable experience. She is a little fighter and continually willing and eager to learn. She has been sitting up unaided since the age of seven months. She can say "dada" and "baba." She has been crawling since she was eight months old and is now continually into everything.

Laura is making excellent progress and at every evaluation has been at the same level as or above other babies in her age group. Of course, we realize we have been lucky. Laura does not seem to be as severely retarded as some children with Down Syndrome are. We hope that she will continue to develop at her present rate, but we do realize her progress could stop or slow down sometime in the future.

This baby that I wanted and have loved from the moment of her conception is a constant delight to me. Her handicap has made her all the more precious to me, and our relationship means more to me than any material possession does or ever will. There is a special closeness between us that makes that little face light up with a smile whenever she catches a glimpse of me. That smile fills me with hope for the future, for a child as full of joy as Laura has so much love to give others.

Her sister and father enjoy her immensely, and she is played with and loved as much as any "normal" child. Her curiosity and delight over newly discovered items are overwhelming. Each accomplishment and new trick is twice as meaningful to us. Laura has, in her short ten months, taught me many valuable lessons. When I stand over her crib at night, I no longer grieve over lost ambitions and goals, for I realize they were not her expectations, they were mine.

The only ambitions I have now for my children are health and happiness. Any other goals will be of their own choosing. I hope they will each develop to their own potential, and as parents we hope we have created the kind of environment whereby that is possible. □

THE STORY OF NATHAN

By Nancy Stock

*"It is difficult to put into words the feelings that enveloped me as
I entered the ICN and was directed to Nathan's isolette.
There lay an incredibly tiny infant, bruised, yellowed with
jaundice, surrounded with wires, tubes, machines, and lights."*

My son, Nathan, recently celebrated his first birthday, and as with all children, it was a sentimental and emotional experience for us. However, my husband and I have a special reason to be thankful for this birthday, because there were so many times we wondered if Nathan would be with us to mark the occasion. For Nathan was a special baby—a baby born ten weeks premature with a host of medical problems. Let me share with you the story of our first year.

On a Sunday evening after a quiet day at home, I began leaking fluid from the vagina. I called my doctor, and after an examination, he confirmed that my water had broken and I was indeed in labor. My pregnancy had been normal to this point, and there had been no forewarning of impending trouble. Since I was ten weeks from the due date, my doctor made arrangements for me to enter Children's Hospital in Buffalo rather than our local hospital where I had intended to deliver. Children's has a neonatal intensive care unit, especially designed for premature infants. Little did we know at the time that the decision to go to Children's probably saved our son's life. Thirty hours later, I gave birth to a 3 lb. 5½ oz. boy with an Apgar score of 2. The doctors told me he was big for his age, but he seemed very tiny to me. A special pediatric team stood by the delivery room and immediately began to work with Nathan.

Nathan's most immediate problem was respiratory, and he needed oxygen and a respirator to breathe. He had hyaline membrane disease (also known as respiratory distress syndrome), a severe lung disorder common in preemies. He was whisked away to the Intensive Care Nursery (ICN) and I (gratefully) was taken to a room in a nonmaternity section of the hospital.

The following morning was my first opportunity to see my son. It is very difficult to put into words the feelings that enveloped me as I entered the ICN and was directed to Nathan's isolette. There lay an incredibly tiny infant, bruised, yellowed with jaundice, surrounded with wires, tubes, machines, and lights. An umbilical line protruded from his navel, an IV cord from his newly shaven head, and tubes from the respirator from his nose. Nathan himself lay there calmly, possibly contemplating the quiet life in the womb from which he had recently emerged.

There were many things I did not notice on my first visit to the ICN: the other babies, approximately 40 in all, also struggling for their lives; the care of the nurses, who gave the babies all the love and compassion they could; and the entire medical staff, working around the clock to give every possible chance for life to these infants. These were all the things I came to observe on subsequent visits to the ICN.

I returned home when Nathan was five days old, with a strange and vacant feeling. A week ago I had been pregnant. Now my pregnancy had terminated, but I didn't actually have a baby either. I had intended to breast-feed my son, and as my milk supply came in and dried up, I was filled with even more feelings of loss. If the doctors had been able to assure us that Nathan would be coming home, perhaps it would have been easier, but that was an assurance no one could make. We lived almost 50 miles from the hospital, and our visits those first few weeks seemed fruitless and depressing. We could not even hold or feed our son. We just stood there and gazed into his isolette, hoping somehow he would be warmed by our presence. To help my emotional state, I returned to my teaching position in an elementary school, and we visited Nathan on evenings and weekends.

Those first long weeks were trying at best. Nathan seemed to slip from one crisis to the next, always rallying in the end. The hospital staff attempted to explain his problems to us, and we would return home at night and look up the complicated terms in a medical book. His condition fluctuated greatly, and he frequently had spells of apnea or bradycardia, where he would stop breathing or his heart rate would slow suddenly. As his condition stabilized, we learned he had two primary problems: severe lung damage due to hyaline membrane disease and a heart defect known as patent ductus arteriosis. When he was six weeks old, he underwent surgery to remove the most severely damaged portion of his right lung in hopes that the remaining lung would expand and grow healthy new tissue. The surgery was successful, and when Nathan was eleven weeks old, his respirator was finally removed, and he breathed his first room air. During those months on the respirator, he had been fed through a nasal tube since the respirator prohibited feeding by mouth. When he was eleven weeks old, I gave him a bottle for the first time with much help and encouragement from his nurse.

When Nathan was three months old, he came home for the first time. I would like to say his homecoming was a wonderful and serene event, but actually I was a bundle of nerves. For three months my son had received highly specialized care, 24 hours a day, and now suddenly he was turned over to me. I felt somewhat 'inadequate to care for a normal newborn, much less a special child. At that point I felt that Nathan belonged more to the nurses than to me. Because of his heart condition, it was necessary for us to check his heart rate frequently and to administer three medications. He often vomited his medications and his food, and we spent many long hours trying to slowly feed him. He had a stomach problem known as chalasia, which caused the vomiting, and we kept him propped up in an infant seat for two hours after each feeding to help counteract this.

Through those first long weeks, my husband was the rock of the family, always calm and patient with Nathan and me. As our lives settled down together, we began to really enjoy our son.

Nathan grew and prospered and became a cheerful baby who always laughed and smiled despite his problems. When he was seven months old, he returned to the hospital for heart surgery. It was successful, but he developed respiratory complications after the surgery, probably due to his previous respiratory problems. What we thought would be a two-week hospital stay dragged out to seven, and it seemed as if our nightmare had come back. Nathan rallied again, and four days before Christmas he arrived home. He was nine months old and weighed 11 pounds.

How is Nathan today? He is a smiling, happy one-year-old. He is bright and alert and has an excellent chance for a normal life. His problems are not completely gone, however. He still has a chronic respiratory condition that requires three therapy sessions a day including the use of an inhalation therapy machine. He is very susceptible to respiratory infections, and we are careful not to expose him unnecessarily. His doctors are confident that his lungs will strengthen and heal in time. Developmentally, at fourteen months, he is crawling, climbing, standing and learning the meaning of "no-no." He weighs 18 pounds and has a cheerful disposition and a bright smile.

How much did all this cost? In all, Nathan spent almost five months in the hospital at a cost of about $50,000. We had excellent hospitalization insurance and are fortunate to live in a state that provides financial assistance for medical bills of special children.

It has been a long and difficult year, and we have many things to be thankful for. Through Nathan we have met other parents of children with problems—many more severe than Nathan's—and all have had the love and courage to see them through. We are grateful to our families and friends who gave us so much support, as well as to the medical staff who made his life possible.

When we chose our son's name during those first long days, we chose Nathan because it means "a gift of the Lord," and we have truly received our gift.